ENSNARED

The drug smugglers who would crush
anyone
in their path to escape justice

By

STEPHEN (BRADSHAW)

BASED ON A TRUE LIFE EXPERIENCE

CONTENTS

FOREWORD

This book is based on an extraordinary sequence of events that took place a little over a decade ago and involved myself, my family, and my colleagues and friends. While most of the narrative is based on fact, I have changed names and various other details to avoid embarrassment to those who were caught up in the story. Some passages are speculative and some are invented, but the basis of the story is true and has not been exaggerated in any way.

I hope the story will make the reader aware of how easy it is for innocent people to be caught up in serious crime through no fault of their own, other than a willingness to trust their fellow human beings.

Stephen (Bradshaw), October 2013

CHAPTER 1

Singapore Airlines flight SQ22 banked sharply to the left, steadied on her course, and quickly broke through the clouds out of Heathrow. It was a glorious sight. No matter how frequently Daniel Cassidy flew, he could not help but marvel at the contrast between the damp, dark, drizzly conditions below and the brilliance of the deep blue sky above. The sun setting on the horizon only added to the moment.

A young couple, perhaps 25 years old, sat to his right, totally absorbed with each other. Since saying a polite hello on boarding, they had not uttered another word in Daniel's direction, preferring to whisper quietly to each other. This suited Daniel fine; he was not one for small talk, and had dreaded the thought of being seated next to someone who would try to spend the entire 13-hour flight giving him their life history.

The drinks trolley headed slowly down the aisle as stewardesses attended it, handing out complimentary drinks and peanuts. Daniel normally restricted his alcohol intake on aircrafts as it tended to worsen the dehydration and headiness he struggled with while flying—something which, at the age of 36, he was taking longer and longer to get over. However, today was different. As the trolley neared, he felt a distinct need to quell the worries that the last trip to London had generated.

"Would you like a drink?" asked the attractive young stewardess dressed elegantly in a long dark blue sarong.

"Gin & tonic, please."

"Ice & lemon?"

"Please."

Daniel reclined his seat the full three inches afforded to him, settled back with his drink, and reflected on his two-week business trip to London. It had been good to catch up with family and friends—without their support; things could have been a damn sight worse. His family home stood in an outstandingly beautiful part of Dorset, and it was always a wonderful retreat. Even under the strain of the last two weeks, he had enjoyed walking the family dogs along the banks of the river, and even found time for a touch of fly-fishing.

His mind slowly refocused on the reality of the situation. Gordon Burrage, the former general manager for his company in the UK, had not been the trustworthy ally and employee both Daniel and his co-owner Luke had thought him to be. In fact, completely the opposite had been true; Gordon had driven the company into the ground, and now Daniel had to pull what was left of it out of the quagmire. Daniel himself was a man of honour, and had naively assumed most others lived by his own standards; something he vowed never to do again.

He had been forced to personally pay off all the debts Burrage had run up in the eight months he had been left in control of the UK company. Given that Gordon knew Daniel had only recently started up a company in Singapore at a significant cost, his final betrayal had been a devastating blow.

Daniel upended the final peanuts from the small foil bag into his mouth, biting down hard as he thought with disgust about how Gordon had been living like a lord for the past few months, travelling everywhere first class and running up huge expenses. It was something neither Daniel nor Luke had ever done, preferring to stick to a tight budget. They should have kept a closer eye on things, they now knew. How wonderful hindsight was!

Daniel's thoughts turned to his dear wife Linda, whom he had phoned just prior to leaving the house. She had offered to collect him from Changi Airport when he landed there the following day, but Daniel had insisted that it was easier to get a taxi and be home in time for drinks on the veranda before dinner.

Daniel flicked on the television set in the backrest of the seat in front, scanning the in-flight guide, *Silverkris*, for the films showing during the flight. He soon spotted two he would like to watch, although he knew from experience that about halfway through the first film a wave of tiredness would kick in, so the chances of him making it awake through both were pretty remote.

He prioritised a Bruce Willis movie to watch straight after dinner had been served, then studied the menu and decided upon the chicken. It arrived about an hour later and, to his surprise, was exceptionally good for an aircraft meal. Within ten minutes of the film starting, true to form, Daniel was asleep with his head propped up against the window.

The next thing he knew was a soft voice asking if he would like breakfast as the lights brightened in the cabin. About an hour later, the captain announced their imminent descent into Singapore's Changi International Airport.

***

About five rows in front of Daniel, a very fit Chinese-Malay gentleman in his mid forties had just finished watching one of the Mandarin movies that had been showing on the flight. He removed his blanket, set aside his headphones, stood, and politely asked the passenger next to him if he would allow him access to the toilet. The man's name was Xu Xiang. As he shuffled out of his seat and wandered back towards the aircraft toilets, he glanced across the aircraft and noted Daniel was absorbed in the Wilbur Smith novel he had been reading in the departure lounge.

This was not the first time Xu had checked up on Daniel; he had been following him since Daniel had alighted from the Jetlink bus at Heathrow's bus terminal. As he watched him, Xu had mused on how perfect Daniel and his company were for the job he and his colleagues had in mind.

***

On the descent, Daniel put his book back into the pocket in front of him and reminisced about the first time he had landed in Singapore with his parents some 25 years earlier. It had been a big upheaval back then, completely uprooting from their farmhouse in Surrey and moving 7000 miles to the unknown. Daniel had endured this with muted enthusiasm at the time, having had to leave all his schoolmates back in the UK, but he'd soon settled into it, and now he found himself living here out of choice.

Daniel's father was an airline pilot who had joined Singapore Airlines back in the mid-seventies as captain of the new DC10 aircraft that were being added to the fleet. During the first year after leaving England, they had spent a considerable amount of time in Long Beach, California, while his father took various refresher courses. It had been a tremendous adventure, and at that age, Disneyland, Universal Studios, Knotts Berry Farm, and Magic Mountain had all been beyond the wildest comprehension of Daniel and his two younger brothers. He remembered thinking that perhaps travelling was not so bad after all.

After much searching, they had settled for a beautiful old colonial house located not far from Daniel's school in a park inhabited entirely by other expatriates. Rochester Park had been built originally for British Army Officers and boasted houses of a good size and sturdy construction with full-length verandas and balconies. They had an *amah*'s quarters, located in a separate bungalow in the garden, and even a small plantation of banana trees. For a growing child, it was paradise.

Daniel's parents had continued to live in Singapore until the early nineties, and the majority of his—and eventually Linda's—Christmases and New Years had been spent in the place he had grown to love dearly.

***

Around him, landing approached, and the stewardesses made the final round for a last check on seat belts. An electric whine and rumble came from the depths of the 747 as the landing gear was lowered, and the couple next to Daniel craned forward to look out of the window to his left. The woman cheerily asked Daniel if it was his first visit.

"No, I've spent a bit of time here. How about you?"

"Oh, it's our first time out of Europe! We're here for a couple of days before we go to see Todd's uncle and aunt in Sydney."

No sooner had Daniel answered a few of their questions about shopping on Orchard Road than the aircraft touched down in a smooth landing Daniel's father would have been proud of. Rain lashed against the aircraft windows as they taxied into the bay, and the severity of it reminded Daniel that this would soon be a daily occurrence when the monsoon winds set in again.

As soon as the pilot applied the brakes and brought the aircraft to a final halt, everyone struggled to grab their luggage from the overhead lockers. Used to this, Daniel had his briefcase at his feet, and would stay seated until the rush subsided.

As the queue to disembark started to move, he wished the couple a good stay, then collected his book from the seat pocket, opened his case, and organised himself for disembarkation.

***

Daniel always marvelled at the splendour and cleanliness of Changi Airport, which had taken over from the old Paya Labar Airport in the eighties. The rows of bougainvillea hanging from the balconied areas gave the whole place a welcoming feel, he had always thought.

As he took the moving walkway towards the arrivals hall, Xu was only about three people behind him, yet Daniel was completely oblivious.

Daniel gave the immigration official a friendly "good evening", but was met with the usual hostile, suspicious, and unfriendly blank look. Daniel had long ago concluded that all immigration officials worldwide must be trained at the same place, with a complete manners bypass. As he stood at the counter, he could recall only a single immigration official, in

Newark, New York, who had actually smiled and bid Daniel a good day in return. What a memorable occasion that was!

CHAPTER 2

Daniel stood at the carousel and waited for his case to come round. As he did so, he glanced beyond Customs to where a crowd of loved ones was forming to meet the arriving passengers. He was looking for Linda. Although he had told her he would get a taxi, she had this knack of occasionally just turning up to meet him, which was always a welcome surprise, though today she had been playing tennis at the club, and unless it had been rained off, she would not have had time.

He concentrated his attention on the baggage belt, which was now a solid stream of cases. He saw his own travelling down the far side, the large security strap in bright colours making the otherwise tatty case impossible to miss. He moved forward to pick it up off the carousel when it reached him, but as he did so, a man moved to pick another case off the line just in front of Daniel's, knocking into Daniel in the process and forcing him to move further down the carousel to retrieve his case.

"I'm sorry," Xu said as Daniel finally retrieved his case. "It wasn't mine anyway".

"Not to worry," Daniel replied with a short smile. Turning away, he made his way towards Customs and the exit.

As expected, Linda was nowhere to be seen, so Daniel made his way to the taxi rank. As he stepped into the warm humid air, he suddenly felt very clammy, and could not wait to get home and change into some shorts and a T-shirt. The 94-degree heat was certainly too much when one was dressed for the English weather.

Yellow-Top taxis waited outside in their dozens; this was a particularly busy time of the day at Changi. Daniel joined the queue, and within minutes was seated in the back of a Toyota Crown taxi while its cheery driver put his case in the boot.

"You go where?" came the voice from the front once the driver had switched on the meter.

"Go to Holland Village, then I'll show you."

Dusk was falling over Singapore as the driver set off down the East Coast Parkway. Even illuminated by harsh streetlights, the roadsides looked simply stunning; an abundance of various colours of bougainvillea and magnificent fan palms lining the route.

Like most local drivers, the taxi driver could not apply a steady throttle. Instead, he pumped the accelerator pedal repeatedly, resulting in three-second intervals of acceleration quickly followed by deceleration that lasted for the entire journey.

As they approached Holland Village, Daniel directed the driver to Dover Road. They then turned into Medway Park, towards Daniel's home. With many of the roads and parks in that area being named after British towns, Daniel often felt patriotism and pride stir within him as he travelled down the familiar streets.

It was approximately 7.30pm when Daniel paid and tipped the driver. As the taxi reversed out of the drive, the porch light illuminated, and the front door of the house opened to reveal Linda's beaming smile. At that moment, it seemed to fill the doorway.

Their home in Medway Park was of a similar construction to the one Daniel had grown up in. It was a large three-bedroomed detached house of a less colonial style than the others, boasting glass windows rather than shutters, but was still substantial, with its own garden and a separate *amah*'s quarters. Gardens were becoming less and less common with the development of all the condominium complexes, but Daniel and Linda had felt that with a child, and the possibility of more on the way, a garden would be an asset. The other feature that had swayed them was a beautiful swimming pool sitting in the shade of a fan palm in the back garden. With the garden backing on to a golf course, the whole area was secluded, and they were not overlooked at all.

As Daniel pushed his case towards her, Linda held on to Skipper, their Alsatian, gripping tightly to his collar as he pulled with anticipation. He wanted to greet Daniel first, as was the ritual every time he returned from a trip.

Linda looked stunning. She was slim, and her off-white slip-ons and white-and-navy shirt accentuated her tan. Daniel's heart missed a beat as he realised yet again how lucky he was to have a wife who was not only very attractive, but completely selfless, fair, and honest. She didn't have a bad word to say about anyone, and Daniel often wondered what he had done to deserve her.

"Hi hon," Linda greeted him. "Good flight?"

"Not too bad sweetheart, how have you been?"

As Daniel reached the door, Linda let Skipper go, and he made the usual fuss. He was not happy until he had been patted, stroked, and talked to for at least two minutes as he whined with happiness, barging between them as Daniel embraced Linda. Skipper eventually calmed down, and Daniel abandoned his case and went through to the veranda.

"What would you like to drink, honey?" Linda called over her shoulder as she disappeared into the kitchen.

"I could slaughter a cold beer. What are you having?"

"I'm having a vodka."

As Linda prepared the drinks, Salvia, their Malay *amah*, appeared to greet Daniel.

"Good evening," she said as she approached the veranda. "You have good trip?"

"Yes thank you Salvia, is all well at this end?"

"Yes sir, although Salim very naughty."

"Oh dear, what has he done this time?"

"He has been very bad to me, sir, but is OK now."

"So long as it is OK now, that's the main thing."

"Yes. You want me to take case up?"

"Please."

Linda walked through from the kitchen, Daniel's beer in hand and ice clinking in her vodka as Salvia disappeared upstairs to unpack the case. They sat down, and Daniel asked after Sam, their two-year-old son.

"He's in bed, absolutely exhausted following his swim this evening," she said. "He just loves the water."

"I shouldn't think it will be long before he's out of armbands, the rate he's going."

"How tired are you, honey?" asked Linda.

"Pretty shattered, it wasn't the easiest of trips." He grinned playfully. "You sound as if you have something in mind?"

"Well, Tom and Mary are in town tonight. It's been suggested that we all go for a Cheap and Cheerful meal. Luke and Michelle are going."

Cheap and Cheerful, as Ghim Moh had become known, was a very basic Chinese eating-house at the base of one of the apartment complexes. Being completely off of the tourist beat, it had become known among many of the expats for its superb but inexpensive cuisine. It was a favourite haunt for Daniel, Linda and their close friends, and was always a must for Daniel's parents when they visited.

"Well, that put pay to any thoughts I had for this evening," Daniel said, raising a brow. "I'd love to see them, although I don't want to be too late. What time should we meet them?"

"About 8.30."

"I'd better get my skates on then, I'll go and shower. I assume Salvia's around?"

"Yes, of course."

Daniel downed the rest of his beer and headed up to shower and change. Linda sat on the end of the bed as he dried off and brought him up to date with some of the events that had occurred during his absence. After Linda had finished explaining the behaviour of Salvia's supposed boyfriend, Daniel suddenly felt less than happy about leaving young Sam in her care, in case Salim was about and started to mistreat Salvia. The abuse had been steadily getting worse over the past few months, and though it was something that Daniel and Linda had tried to stay out of, it sounded as if it would soon be time for some intervention.

After Linda assured Daniel that Salim would not be about that evening as he was working, he agreed to go as planned.

CHAPTER 3

Once Daniel was ready, they told Salvia they were off, advised her that they would not be late, and walked to their Mitsubishi Galant. Daniel got into the passenger side as Linda unlocked the doors, and they headed off for the five-minute journey to Holland Village and Ghim Moh.

"How's the car?" asked Daniel.

"Fine, although I think it's due for a service shortly."

"I'll book it in in the next few days."

Daniel was still reeling from the purchase of their car. In the UK, it would have cost about £15,000, while in Singapore it had cost him the equivalent of over £40,000. The car was on finance over a five-year period, but even that was a hefty amount to find each month.

Daniel's mind went to the problems they were facing with the UK business, and the fact that they would soon have to start propping it up personally. They would also have to find new products to help it recover. As they approached Ghim Moh, Daniel tried to push that train of thought away. It would only depress him, and he wanted to enjoy his evening.

He was cheered the moment they rounded the corner and saw Mary, Tom, Colin, Luke, and Michelle all having a good laugh at one of Mary's many jokes. Daniel and Linda greeted them fondly, sat down, and began to join in with the banter and jollities of the evening.

Luke had kept the seat next to him for Daniel, with whom he had talked just prior to leaving London. Even so, he was dying to get a full rundown on the situation.

"All OK?" he asked.

"As good as can be expected under the circumstances."

Daniel gave Luke a brief rundown on the last conversation he had had with Gordon and just how little he had achieved for his salary and the expenses he had drawn. Neither Luke nor Daniel could understand the man's thinking.

"It was as if he wanted to take us for as much as he could," Luke commented.

"Yes" Daniel agreed. "It crossed my mind, but it's not as if he was able to throw away a £60,000-a-year job. I simply don't understand it."

"Have you changed the locks to the offices and warehouse?"

"Yes, and I've told Louise that if he shows up at the office, he is not to be let in under any circumstances. I told her to get the warehouse manager to help her if she has any trouble."

"Do you think he's likely to create a scene then?"

"Well, he took his dismissal less than honourably. He said it would be the end of him, and asked if we wanted that on our consciences."

"What's he on about? He can't be that hard up. Looking at his CV and previous salaries, he could almost afford to retire by now."

"As I pointed out to him, if we let him run the company for any longer, it would be the end of us. Just when things are finally heading in the right direction, along comes another bloody great spanner and jams up the works!"

"Come on chaps, I hope you're not talking shop?" came Michelle's voice from the other side of the table.

Daniel smiled and scanned his menu. "The chilli crab is your favourite, isn't it, Mary?"

"I've been salivating at the thought of it for months!" came the reply.

Daniel turned back to Luke briefly. "I'll be having a lie-in in the morning, but are you in the office tomorrow afternoon?"

"No, I've got a meeting at 2pm at the Pan Pacific with the Shanghai factory rep."

"How about the Tanglin Club at six?"

"Yeah, fine."

"I'll reserve a table in the Churchill Room for dinner."

As Luke ordered with the waitress, Daniel greeted Colin, sat to Luke's right. He had been a family friend of Daniel and Linda's for many years, and was responsible for putting Daniel in touch with Luke. Both men had been living in Singapore working for other companies, but on meeting at one of Colin's yearly Christmas parties, they had started to discuss the future. They had uncannily similar views, and shared the ambition of running their own business. They had turned this ambition into a reality two years ago with the backing of their wives, both handing in their notices to their respective companies on the same day. Their leisure and marine business had turned in better figures than expected during its first eighteen months of trading, but equally the costs were higher than anticipated. All in all, however, things were not far off track.

After exchanging pleasantries, both Colin and Daniel turned their attentions back to the table.

"How's the credit card Tom, is it in meltdown yet?" Luke asked. "Or hasn't Mary been here long enough to give it a good pasting?"

The response came from Mary. "I came with great expectations, and I've been out today to 'shop till you drop', but I simply couldn't find anything I liked," she said. "Tom couldn't believe it."

"Still managed to spend over a thousand dollars though," came the wry reply from her husband.

"Tom's promised to buy me the most beautiful pair of earrings I saw in Dubai on the way out. He's going to treat me to them on the way home, aren't you Thomas? I saw a similar pair in London just before coming out, and they were about twice the price, so with that sort of saving, he just can't afford not to!"

"What's on the cards for tomorrow, Mary?" Daniel asked.

"Well, we'd like to go and see the old house in Rochester Park, then do a trip to Holland Village before preparing for tomorrow evening's flight."

"I'm planning to collect them from the Shangri La at about 9.30, then we'll see how the day takes us," said Linda helpfully. "We'll probably head back about tea time before taking them to the airport tomorrow evening."

"OK, honey. I won't be able to make the airport trip; I've got to catch up on everything with Luke."

As they finished their meal, Daniel turned to Linda and gave her a look that said he was tired and wanted to make a move. She recognised it immediately, and knew how exhausted he must be, so suggested running Tom and Mary back to the hotel before making their way home.

On arrival at the Shangri La, Tom offered Linda and Daniel a nightcap; more out of courtesy than anything else, as he had noticed that Daniel was nearly asleep in the back of the car. Linda politely declined and headed home. She would almost need to carry her husband to bed.

CHAPTER 4

Xu Xiang had followed Daniel through passport control and seen him get into a taxi. He watched more out of curiosity than anything else, as he knew only too well where he was going. Xu and his colleagues had learned everything there was to know about Daniel Cassidy and his family, and indeed Luke Oakley and his—they had done their homework since first targeting them six months earlier.

Xu made his way to the pick-up point just as Han Atima drew up in Xu's White Mercedes S280. Xu saw him coming, picked up his bag, and got into the passenger seat of the Merc without acknowledging him. Han took off, forcing an unsuspecting taxi driver to brake heavily as he did so. This was not the first time Han's extravagant driving style had caused trouble; a few weeks earlier, he had tried an impossible manoeuvre and ended up with a long deep gouge down the right hand side of the car.

They passed the control tower and were heading down the East Coast Parkway before Han said, "How's it been left?"

"They have sacked the stupid bastard."

"Justified?"

"Oh it was justified all right, he was getting greedy. I'd have done the same in their position."

They continued to the Shaw Centre on the corner of Orchard and Scotts Road, where they parked in the multi-storey and made their way up to their 12th floor office. The heading above the door read 'United European Marine Ltd'. It was a single large room, with a small glass-walled office in one corner.

UEM Ltd had rented the office for a six-month period only two weeks previously. They had had decorators in continuously since then, and had turned an ordinary room into a plush office with thick Wilton carpeting, a leather suite, expensive coffee tables and solid rosewood desks. The photocopier and fax machine sat in the glass office along with newly-printed headed paper and business cards, but very little else.

Han unlocked the door, flicked the light switch, and went to sit down. Xu broke open a bottle of Courvoisier from a minibar off to one side and joined Han in another of the luxurious leather armchairs.

"Looks good," Han remarked.

"It'll do the job," Xu commented, handing him a cognac.

"Just needs some pictures now."

"Have you brought them with you?"

"Yes, I'll take them downtown for framing tomorrow."

The pictures Han had rolled up in his case were of an assortment of sports boats. They had been doctored before he left Turkey that day to eliminate any manufacturers' markings or names that might have shown, and to change a few details. The results weren't perfect, but they would do the job. Time was not on their side.

"Yes, if you do that, I'll collect them when they're ready," said Xu. "If you give me the negatives, I'll also get the brochure completed. In light of the situation, I am going to try and make contact with Daniel or Luke in the next day or so. You need to go to London and deal with Burrage. He's claiming the fee for what he's done so far, and he's going to talk to Daniel and the authorities if he doesn't get it."

"I think that idiot has just pushed his luck too far. I'll try and get a flight out tomorrow."

They spoke about their next steps for another half an hour, then decided to call it a day. They locked the office, got the lift down to the car park, and set off to Xu's home in Clementi. He woke his amah the moment he got into the apartment, demanding she make them both a meal and ready the guest room for Han. The frail-looking Filipina duly jumped up and obeyed.

CHAPTER 5

The advertisement in the Daily Telegraph had read:

General Sales Manager required for expanding Marine Leisure company based in Surrey. Offers friendly team and good benefits, inc. £60,000 p.a., company car, and expenses. Candidate must have previous marine experience, be a good communicator, and able to lead.

Having seen the writing on the wall in his current company, Gordon Burrage had decided to apply. He knew he was on the shortlist for the chop, as he had been unable to hide his drinking problem from them for long. They had put up with it for some time without mentioning anything, but it was getting worse, now affecting not only his performance, but his attendance. He knew it was only a matter of time.

He had sent his CV off, and before long received a response inviting him to the company's office for an interview. Daniel and Luke had interviewed him, explaining that the UK arm of their company had expanded to a stage where it could no longer be run remotely. Their sales staff and office administrators did a fine job, but they needed a consistent leader who was there all the time. They told him they had interviewed five possible candidates, but Gordon was the one they had settled on.

He had been very keen on the thought of being left solely in charge. With nobody looking over his shoulder, his drinking would surely remain undiscovered. In fact, he reasoned, his successful application was a good justification for him to celebrate with a drink when he returned home that night.

Gordon's wife had left him a year or so earlier; pushed over the edge by his alcoholism. Gordon refused to blame it; their marriage had already been on pretty rocky ground following her discovery that her husband had been seen with a prostitute on one of his business trips by a colleague of hers who happened to be in Amsterdam the same week. It had been extremely unfortunate for him, and even his friends had agreed it was rotten luck.

Han Atima had befriended him about six months before, during one of his regular evening drink binges, and had continued to bump into him 'coincidentally' for several days afterwards.

When they discussed the marine industry, Han reckoned he had an offer that would make Gordon a hero with his bosses. The profit this venture would generate enabled him to guarantee Gordon £100,000 commission in cash from Han's company.

Gordon had sobered up immediately at the thought, and had given Han his undivided attention. With the realisation that so much easy money would be coming his way in the near future, along with the ego boost of securing a new product line-up, he had increased his spending, both of personal funds the company's. Over time, he became complacent, and soon the drinking was clearly visible alongside his new happy-go-lucky attitude.

Louise had voiced her concerns to Luke after a few months, and started to make notes, promising she would let Daniel know what was happening on his next visit.

On his return to the office, Daniel had had a lengthy meeting with Louise and the warehouse management, taking on board what they had to say. Upon looking at the latest finances, he had been horrified. In the previous three-month period, there had been no fewer than eight first-class flights to Germany, Italy, Spain and Portugal, all accompanied by further lavish expenses at five-star hotels.

After consulting Luke, Daniel had sacked him. Gordon had not taken it well, and had begged to keep his job. It had been a pitiful sight to see a man of his age dissolving into such a state of distress so readily, but Daniel had to stick to the decision.

CHAPTER 6

Han had managed to get an Emirates flight back to London the day after the meeting with Xu. He'd had a couple of days to think about how to handle Gordon and his blackmail, and had come up with the perfect answer.

Once he had landed, Han got the hotel courtesy bus from Terminal 3 to the Forte hotel, where he started to put the plan in motion. His first call was to Chan, one of Xu's contacts in London. Xu had already sent him a message to keep time free for Han, so once he explained what had to be done, they arranged things for the very next day.

Han then called Gordon, who had eagerly been expecting his pay-off, or at least a portion of it, as silencing money. Although Gordon didn't know the full extent of Han's plans, he felt sure that he must have earned something for what he had done so far. Gordon was deeply annoyed with himself for having been sacked and consequently being unable to earn the full amount, but what did he have to lose by requesting it?

Gordon's resolve steeled as his phone rang.

"It's Han. I've spoken to my boss about your money. They want me to meet you to talk it through."

"I wouldn't have expected anything less."

"I'll meet you tomorrow night at the Hatch pub on the outskirts of Dorking."

"What time?"

"About 9pm, I have some other business to tidy up first."

"See you then."

Gordon rubbed his hands in anticipation. Surely his lack of involvement wouldn't matter to Han or the others? With profit guaranteed, the boat deal would still go through, and everyone would be happy.

***

The following evening, after many phone calls during the day about their strategy, Chan pulled his rented Mondeo into the Forte hotel where Han was waiting for him. Han hopped in, and they drove to Leatherhead for a good meal and to finalise their game plan. Chan knew better than to ask what all this was about; as his orders to follow Han were a direct instruction from Xu, there would be no hesitation from him.

They arrived at the rendezvous at exactly 8.45pm, parked the Mondeo in a dark corner of the car park, and waited. At 9.10, Gordon arrived, late as always, and probably half-drunk already, from the way he swung his Jaguar into the parking spot. They sat and watched as he entered the bar, where they had decided to leave him to keep drinking, particularly as he would be nervous about the meeting.

***

Gordon looked around as he entered the bar, but could see no sign of Han. His first priority was to order a whisky to fortify his nerves and resolve to stand up for what he wanted. In truth, he had already been drinking heavily all afternoon, and by the time he had downed his fourth double whisky, he was becoming drunk even by his standards.

Chan went into the bar at about 9.30pm and noted that Gordon was propped up on one of the bar stools. As it was a weekday, there were very few people in the pub; only a few gaggles seated at tables around the edge. Gordon was the only person who was actually sitting at the bar, deep in conversation with the barman. Chan went up to the bar a pace or so away from where he sat, and ordered a pint of Tennants. As he approached, he gathered the gist of the conversation with the barman—his current sob story.

Chan smiled to himself. *Perfect.*

One of the other customers came up to the far end of the bar to order a round of drinks, and when the barman left to serve him, Gordon decided to head out to the gents'. While the barman's back was turned, Chan seized his opportunity and emptied a small quantity of powder into Gordon's glass, watching it dissolve. He knew that in the state Gordon was, it would not take much to knock him out.

Moments later, Gordon returned and regained his stance at the bar. Within a couple of minutes, the barman had finished with the other order and headed back in his direction. Chan moved away to a side table to sit and observe. Predictably, Gordon emptied his glass in minutes and began to order another.

"Shall I book you a taxi?" the barman asked with a concerned frown.

"If my friend doesn't turn up, you might have to," admitted Gordon.

Chan used his mobile to text Han a report of the situation and layout of people in the pub. Within a few moments, Han put his head round the door and addressed one of the tables of people nearby. Gordon, who chatted with the barman some distance away, could not see him.

"Any of you people got a Jaguar in the car park? You've left your lights on."

Without waiting for an answer, he quickly departed back outside and waited.

One of the guys at the table got up and walked towards the bar, stopping by Chan on the way to ask if he had a Jag in the car park. When the reply was negative, he informed the barman that a Jaguar was sitting in the car park with its lights on.

"It's not yours, is it?" the barman asked, looking in Gordon's direction.

"What's not mine?" Gordon was by now lost in the depths of drunkenness.

"A Jaguar. In the car park?"

"Oh, yeah...why?"

The barman looked at the man who had informed him, raised his eyebrows, and thanked him. He looked back at Gordon.

"Your lights are on. Not that that will worry you tonight." he muttered, knowing he was going to have to call a taxi for this particular customer.

"I'll switch them off."

"OK sir, you do that and I'll phone for a taxi for you."

Gordon stumbled his way towards the door and out into the fresh air.

"Evening, Gordon!" Han greeted him just outside the door. "Follow me and we'll have our chat."

Gordon was by now almost beyond knowing who Han was, but let himself be guided to the Mondeo, where he sat in the passenger seat. He was rapidly becoming more and more drowsy, and within two minutes his head had lolled forwards and he was out cold. Han pulled on a pair of gloves, felt Gordon's pockets, and recovered his car keys. He got out of the Mondeo, leaving its keys in the door pocket, checked that there was nobody else around, and walked to the Jaguar. He let himself in and fired the engine up, revving it unnecessarily. He put the car into reverse and planted his foot to the floor. The tyres screeched mercilessly as the Jaguar's rear wheels lost traction on the smooth car park surface. Han engaged drive and gunned the engine to as he pulled onto the road. As he turned a sharp left out of the car park, he accelerated hard onto the main road, the wheels screeching loudly. He passed the front of the pub at speed, and then backed off and drove sedately to the rendezvous.

The barman had been on the phone to the local taxi dispatcher when he heard the shriek of burning rubber in the car park and sighed.

"Sorry, cancel that booking, he's just left," he said down the phone.

Chan left it three or four minutes before he thanked the barman and made his way to the car park. He got into the Mondeo, retrieved the keys from the door, buckled Gordon into his seat, and headed off in the same direction as the Jaguar.

Chan caught up with Han in the car park of one of the local beauty spots, Leith Hill. The car park was fairly small with an unfinished gravel surface, and it was dark and deserted, as expected. Han reversed the Jaguar into one of the corners where the back of the car was facing the trees and killed the lights. Within four minutes, the pair were heading back to London in the Mondeo. They had not seen another soul.

CHAPTER 7

Linda got up quietly the next morning, leaving Daniel in the land of nod. She went into Sam's room to find him playing quietly with his toys. His little face lit up as he saw Linda, and he held his arms out to be picked up. Linda dressed him and took him downstairs, where Salvia had laid out breakfast on the marble veranda table. Sam's high chair stood next to Linda's normal seat.

Breakfast was a wonderful occasion in the Cassidy household; the family loved sitting in the fresh air with honeydew melons, papaya, and freshly squeezed orange juice, as well as croissants and a pot of tea. Linda's favourite breakfast was diced papaya with fresh lemon and a sprinkling of sugar, which she had just finished when she realised that she would have to go to collect Tom and Mary.

"Salvia, we're off now, but will be back for lunch with two friends," she called. "They will be here for the day before going to the airport tonight."

"OK, two friends, Ma'am. Where's Sir?"

"He's still in bed. Don't disturb him, he's very tired."

"He have lunch too, Ma'am?"

"Yes please. See you later."

"You take Sam?"

"Yes, Sam's coming with me this morning."

***

A short drive later, Linda drew up at the Shangri La, where Mary and Tom were waiting.

"Do you mind if we pop into town first?" Mary asked. "There are a couple of things I would like to get at CK Tangs before we leave."

"Sure. You know me, Mary, I welcome the opportunity to shop!"

They parked in the Shaw Centre car park, which was central for most things. Linda got the pushchair out of the boot and fastened Sam into it. Within minutes, they had locked the car and were on their way.

First, they crossed Scotts Road and went into CK Tang. Tom opted to go off on his own for a while, so they arranged to meet at a coffee shop on the corner next to the Dynasty Hotel at 11.30.

Linda had a wonderful morning. She enjoyed having friends from the UK around, and as they approached the coffee shop she realised that neither she nor Mary had stopped talking for the entire hour. Tom was already seated, but when he saw them coming he got up and went to order three cappuccinos and a selection of Danish pastries.

Once settled, Linda updated them on life in Singapore. After all the upheaval of Daniel and Luke starting the new business, it was at last beginning to take on a sense of normality and routine. It was a comforting feeling, but she admitted that she couldn't go through all that stress and worry again any time soon. Brightly, she turned her attention back to the visiting couple to ask if they had done everything they set out to.

"I'm dying to see the house in Rochester Park," Mary commented.

"I'm not so sure you'll appreciate what you find," Linda warned her, "But we'll go now, before we head back for lunch." With that, they left the coffee shop and headed back to the car.

***

Returning from Tom and Mary's former home, they approached the Cassidy family house in the opposite direction to normal, and Linda saw a large white Mercedes stopped in the road outside their neighbour's house. She only noticed it because of the awkward way it was parked on the verge and the fact that there was someone sitting at the wheel. She was sure it hadn't been there when she left, but dismissed it.

Probably someone's driver, she thought.

Daniel was up when they arrived home. He had been working in his study on his laptop, but joined the others on the veranda for a glass of wine before eating. As soon as they had finished lunch, Daniel changed and bid goodbye to Tom and Mary, who were going to spend the afternoon relaxing by the pool before going to the airport that evening. As he turned to go, Linda stood up.

"I'll run you to the office, honey," she said.

"Are you sure? Why don't you relax here with Mary and Tom?"

"They'll be quite happy on their own for an hour or so, I'm sure."

Daniel agreed, and as they reversed out of the drive, Linda caught a glimpse of the front corner of the white Mercedes, still in the neighbour's drive. As they drove away, the Mercedes edged out and started to follow.

**

Xu knew that he had to move quickly. Without Gordon assisting with the formalities of the deal, they were going to have to cajole Daniel or Luke in the right direction themselves. He had to find a way of introducing himself and getting things underway, and promptly.

He followed the Mitsubishi to the entrance of Daniel and Luke's office in the Golden Mile tower on Beach Road, where he saw Daniel kiss Linda goodbye and head into the office. Xu parked in a public car park opposite the office complex, and again settled in to wait. He sat at a table in a small old-fashioned shop house near Arab Street and had a sweet, thick coffee as he made conversation with the elderly Chinese owner, who was dressed in a scruffy singlet vest, shorts, and flip flops. After the man had left, Xu pretended to read a paper and followed the coffee with root beers, never taking his eyes off the main doors to the office block for more than a second or two at a time.

***

Daniel and Luke's office on the 23rd floor boasted beautiful panoramic views over the harbour. This had been the main selling point, especially to Luke, who particularly enjoyed the sea. He had insisted that as they spent so much time in the office it might as well be a pleasant environment. That said, it was not lavishly or expensively furnished, but practical and comfortable.

As Daniel arrived, Vera, their secretary, greeted him and thrust a handful of messages in his direction, stating that the top three were urgent. Daniel settled himself at his desk and went through them, following up on those that were of immediate importance. As he did, Vera made him a cup of tea and started to bring him up to date with the office events over the past couple of weeks.

At about 5.30, Xu saw Daniel leave the building and stand in the road to hail a taxi. He made haste back to the Mercedes, fired it up and edged it into the road so that he could follow as soon as Daniel had succeeded in getting a taxi. The cab arrived at the Tanglin Club at 5.56pm, and Daniel headed straight for the bar. Xu passed the cab as

Daniel got out, and followed the road to the back of the building and the car park.

When Daniel had first arrived in Singapore, The Tanglin Club had been a place of tremendous character; an old colonial construction built on stilts, as most of the buildings of that era had been. As a child, he had spent many an hour in the pool while his parents had socialised at the bar. He remembered it closing for the reconstruction and the impressive transformation. The club now had a grand main entrance and elegant marble-clad lobby, but had sadly lost some of its relaxed charm. It was, however, still a good watering hole for the expatriate community.

Xu had recently joined the club as a temporary member. He would have to have been on the waiting list for years for full membership, but temporary access was all he needed to give him the short-term credibility he required. He made his way to the bar.

Daniel had ordered a beer and was standing at the bar waiting for Luke when Xu walked in. He stood close to Daniel, and seeing what he was drinking, also ordered a beer. He made a point of looking quizzically in Daniel's direction for several moments until he caught his eye.

"Excuse me, but haven't you recently arrived from London?" Xu asked.

Daniel looked at Xu with faint recognition. "As a matter of fact, I have," he said.

"I thought I recognised you. I'm embarrassed to admit it, but I bumped into you while I was trying to get my luggage from the conveyor at the airport."

"Oh, yes of course!" Daniel said with a smile.

"I'm Edward Lim," said Xu, offering a hand.

"Good to meet you, Edward. Daniel Cassidy."

"I am sorry about that business at the airport. Getting my case off the conveyor from among the other baggage was not easy."

"Don't worry, no harm done."

"Have you been in Singapore long?"

"On and off for many years. How about you?"

"Yes, born and bred," lied Xu.

"I haven't seen you at the club before. Have you belonged for a long time?"

"Yes, quite a while, but I don't use my membership that often. I spend a large portion of my time in Europe."

"Really, whereabouts in Europe?" asked Daniel.

"Well, I have a branch of my business in Istanbul, Turkey."

"What line of work are you in?"

"I have a number of interests, but my main one in Europe is boat building."

"Really! What sort of boats are you involved with?"

"We manufacture small sports boats and Scarab-style power boats. Have you ever encountered one?"

"Well, what a coincidence! I'm actually involved with boats of that type myself."

"Really?" Xu responded with a genuine look of surprise. "Do you manufacture?"

"We design and market; the manufacturing is subcontracted to various UK companies."

"Oh I see. So you sell in the UK?" said Xu, knowing perfectly well how Daniel's organisation was set up.

"Yes. The marine side of our business trades in the UK and Continental Europe, while our leisure business markets to both Asia and Europe."

"Oh I see! This must be fate!"

"What's your set-up?" Daniel inquired.

"My partner and I have a number of interests in Europe, including a boat manufacturing plant in Turkey. We can produce beautifully finished boats for about a third of the cost of production in the UK. We design and develop new models all the time, as well as building to spec for customers like yourselves."

"That's very interesting. I must say, you never know who you're going to bump into in this place. I thought my line of work was pretty unique here!" Daniel remarked with a smile.

"Maybe we should get together and have a longer chat at some stage. Do you have a card?"

"Sure, I would be interested in doing that." Daniel dug a card out of his wallet, and Xu duly produced a card from his introducing 'Mr Edward Lim, CEO United European Marine Ltd', and handed it to Daniel with both hands and a slight bow, something Daniel reciprocated. Xu was pleased to note Daniel's card detailed his office details both in the UK and Singapore.

At that moment, Luke walked into the bar and headed for where Daniel and Xu were standing. He wandered up between them and patted Daniel on the shoulder.

"What can I get you?"

"Oh, hi mate. Let me introduce you to Edward Lim. Believe it or not, he's another boat manufacturer. Edward, this is my partner in crime, Luke Oakley."

"Pleased to meet you Luke," Xu said brightly.

"Likewise."

Luke asked the barman for a beer and grabbed a handful of complimentary nuts off of the bar. "Shall we find a table?" he asked.

"Sure" said Daniel. "Would you excuse us, Edward? I'm afraid that having been away, there's a lot I need to catch up on."

"Fine. It's been good to meet you; perhaps we can meet again in the near future to see if we have any common ground on which to do business."

"Are you in town for a while?"

"Only this week. Could we meet towards the end of it?"

"If you give me a bell in the office tomorrow, we should be able to sort something out. If I'm not there, Vera has my diary, and I'll ask her to pencil something in."

"That would be fine. Have a good evening. It was good to meet you too, Mr Oakley."

Daniel and Luke each shook his hand and wandered to a table.

"Fancy bumping into another boat builder; and one from my flight back from London as well!" Daniel commented as they walked off.

Xu finished his drink and promptly left the club as Daniel brought Luke up to date with all the happenings in the UK, including a detailed account of Gordon's dismissal.

"He took it far worse than I had imagined," Daniel said. "He was literally begging me not to dismiss him, to let him have a second chance. Anyone would have thought it was a matter of life and death."

"A second chance, after the way he'd behaved? He must have been joking!"

"Our table will be ready in the Churchill Room by now, shall we go and eat?"

They walked across the beautiful marble lobby to the Churchill Room, where they were greeted at the door and shown to their table. Once they were seated and had ordered their meals, Luke opened up the conversation again.

"Have you had any further ideas to keep the business in the UK on the straight and narrow? I think we need to do something, particularly in light of the Gordon situation."

Daniel took a sip of the house Merlot that had just been poured, and studied the ruby liquid before responding.

"I don't think we have any option other than to view the lack of a general manager as a temporary setback, and continue on the same tack as before."

"If that's the case, when should we think about the trip to the US to view that new range we're looking at?"

"Well, we're going to need to discuss things with the manufacturers if we're going to have an idea of what we're doing for the London Boat Show in January, but perhaps we could go on to South Carolina after it?"

"What about that guy you were just talking to, would it be worth seeing what he has to offer before we venture to the States?"

"If he rings tomorrow, we'll see him this week, but let's crack on with the US manufacturer anyhow. We need to expand the range with products that complement what we have already."

"OK, I'll get that in motion. It'll be good to be in the office for a change."

They spent the rest of the meal discussing how the leisure branch was performing, and how to improve its productivity. Luke was in the middle of designing a new product along the lines of their previous discussions, and brought Daniel up to date with the samples that were currently being made for them.

They left together shortly after finishing their dessert of apple pie and ice cream—something for which Luke had a weakness, and had insisted upon ordering. They shared a taxi to Daniel's house, and Luke carried on home from there. They would continue their discussions in the office the following day.

CHAPTER 8

Linda returned from dropping Daniel at the office to join Mary and Tom around the pool before they went to shower and change ready for the journey back to the UK. Once changed, they had a cup of tea on the veranda, with Mary lavishing much attention on Sam, who was delighted by it.

They left the house at about six to head off to the airport. There was much chatter in the car as Mary and Tom discussed all that they needed to get on with when they got home. It became obvious that Mary was angling for a new kitchen; something that Tom was less than enthusiastic about, Linda noted with a laugh.

She had decided not to go into the airport terminal, as she hoped that Daniel wouldn't be too late home and was looking forward to spending some time with him. As they stood at the drop-off point, Tom removed their cases from the boot and Linda reminded Mary that they would all be back in the UK for Christmas that year, and that as Daniel would be at the London Boat Show at Earls Court, they could perhaps go sale shopping in January. This was something Mary said she wouldn't miss for the world.

Linda was back in the house by 8pm. Salvia had supper ready for her, having already put young Sam to bed. Linda tried ringing Daniel's mobile to find out what time he would be home, but when the automated voice told her to leave a message, she realised that they were obviously still in the club—the use of mobiles was banned there.

She was nearly asleep in front of the television when Daniel finally arrived home at about 10.30. They sat up for a couple of hours and had a nightcap as Linda recounted her day's events. Daniel in turn told Linda of everything that had been going on that evening, including his chance meeting with Edward Lim, who he explained could well be of assistance to them in the manufacturing of Scarab-style boats in Turkey.

"It all seems very coincidental," Linda remarked. "Particularly as you're looking for that type of boat at the moment."

"Yes, I thought so too," he acknowledged, "but life is full of coincidences, and if you don't make the most of these things, you could well end up losing out."

Linda yawned and squeezed Daniel's hand. "I think it's time for bed."

He grinned mischievously. "I hope you're not thinking of sleep for a while!"

***

The following day, life begun to get back to normal, with Daniel and Linda getting up at seven and enjoying their morning cup of tea in bed, Sam playing at their feet. They chatted, and both agreed that perhaps things were at last looking up, and that life might be a little less stressful from now on.

Following breakfast, Daniel got a taxi into work and Linda started to go about her normal routine, which today would consist of a swim at the polo club's pool, followed by coffee with some friends in Sunset Heights.

*****

Daniel was sitting at his desk when Luke arrived, and they both dug into their in-trays. Little was said for the first half an hour. At about 10am the phone rang. Vera answered it in the normal way, informing Daniel before putting them through.

"It's a Mr Lim for you Daniel, are you in?"

"Yes, fine Vera, thanks."

He picked up the phone. "Good morning Edward! I hadn't expected to hear from you this early, I thought you'd still be jetlagged."

Lim laughed. "I got used to feeling lousy from jetlag ages ago. Now I just live with it. Anyhow, how about our meeting? Can you make it tomorrow? I have to leave town earlier than expected, but I'm sure you'll be interested in what we do."

"Sure, I can fit that in. What sort of time did you have in mind?"

"How about 2pm? Can you make it to my office?"

"The Shaw Centre, isn't it?" Daniel asked, remembering the address on his card. "Yes, I can be there for two."

"Two o'clock it is then," said Lim. "I look forward to seeing you tomorrow. Goodbye."

A while later, Luke remembered that he had promised to take Michelle out to lunch with some friends visiting from Kuala Lumpur the next day.

"That's OK," Daniel said. "I'll go, and report back. It's probably a wild goose chase anyway."

The pair spent the rest of the day sorting out the backlog of work that had built up, and it was not until Vera asked if there was anything else they would like her to do before she departed that they both realised how late it had become. Daniel did not want to be late home that night, and left shortly afterwards. He hoped to have a swim with Sam before he went to bed, followed by a quiet evening at home with his wife. Luke announced that he would stay on in the office for a short while, insisting that he had to finish a new specification to send to a manufacturer in China before he left.

Daniel knew only too well that Luke's 'short while' would probably last until midnight. He had been misled many times by Luke's concept of 'five minutes', usually at five o'clock when they planned to go for a drink, and would arrive at the bar just in time for last orders. He now knew better, but Michelle, who spent a lot of time with Linda, was becoming increasingly uptight with Luke's working hours and habits; something with which Daniel and Linda could sympathize. Rarely did Daniel interfere, except for the odd occasion when Linda would ask him to get Luke home at a reasonable time, or tell him that she had had a reminder from Michelle that it was their anniversary. Michelle tried to remind herself that that 'was just the way he was', and that she wouldn't want it any other way.

It had been pouring with rain again that afternoon, only just stopping as Daniel arrived home in the taxi. As he got out, he could hear frogs croaking from somewhere within the large storm drains that ran round the houses. Steam rose off the driveway as the late evening sunlight evaporated the water on the tarmac.

It had been Salvia's afternoon off, and Linda was preparing roast lamb for supper while Sam played with his toys on the dining room floor. His face lit up as he saw his father walk in. Daniel picked him up, gave him a kiss, and suggested a swim, which Sam happily accepted. They swam and played in the pool while Linda finished preparing the supper, and Skipper lay asleep under the ceiling fan on the veranda.

As they ate and enjoyed a bottle of Barramundi, Daniel suggested that the following night they should go out to Jumbo Seafood, a favourite restaurant of theirs on the East Coast Parkway. Linda thought this was an excellent idea; it would make a change from the restaurants they had been frequenting on Boat Quay.

CHAPTER 9

Daniel arrived at the offices of United European Marine Ltd at 2.05pm the next day, having spent the entire morning in the office, bar a brief stop for a sandwich at the deli on Scotts Road on the way there. He pushed the button on the intercom to the left of the door. After a few seconds, he heard a buzz and the latch releasing. He pushed open the door and went in to be greeted by a young Chinese receptionist. She offered him a seat in one of the fine leather armchairs.

"Can I get you a coffee or green tea?"

"Green tea would be lovely, thank you."

Daniel stood and wandered round the room, looking at the pictures of boats that adorned the walls. They certainly offered an assortment of styles and models, although Daniel's initial thoughts were that those on show did not follow any particular theme. Usually, with boat manufacturers, there was a general trend in the styling, but these boats were all very different. Indeed, if he had not been informed otherwise, he would have said that different companies had manufactured them. Some of the boats had flat sterns, some were canoe-sterned, and some had shaved-off sleek sterns. Some offered sleek cutting entries to the water with drooped bows, while others were blunt with raised bows.

Daniel guessed that these were probably a cross-section; one model from each range each destined for different markets. If this was the case, the firm must be a substantial manufacturer. There were certainly some models on the wall fitted their requirements exactly.

Maybe this wasn't a wild goose chase after all, Daniel thought to himself, his spirits lifting.

The receptionist, who had prepared the tea in a small office in the corner, walked back in to advise Daniel that Mr Lim would only be a couple of minutes. He sat back down, his mind already racing with thoughts of what they could do with some of these products. Mr Lim's entry into Daniel and Luke's lives could not have been timed better.

Edward Lim arrived shortly afterward. In reality, he had been waiting round the corner to give his guest time to have a good look at the products they supposedly had on offer.

"Good afternoon Daniel, I see you found us all right!"

"Yes thank you Edward."

"Welcome to our humble office. Please do sit down."

"It's very smart and tasteful," Daniel replied.

"Just like our boats!" Lim replied with a laugh.

Over cups of green tea, they chatted briefly about their respective businesses. Lim advised Daniel that he and his European partner produced about 2000 boats a year, most of which were models of their own design. They were looking for a UK importer for their boats, and were keen to get the product moving by early the following season.

"Are you actively looking for new products to import?" asked Lim. "Or maybe we can be of assistance with manufacturing your current models in our factory? We can produce very cheaply thanks to the low cost of labour in Turkey."

"Well, we are looking for products to complement our existing range of boats," replied Daniel. "We're mainly involved with the sailing market at the moment, but we're keen to diversify into the power market with 18 to 28 foot sports boats initially, and see where it goes from there. I don't think transferring the building of our racing sailboats is really a feasible option, as the volume is not particularly high and the construction and weights are critical, but the importation of some models like this would certainly be of interest."

As Daniel said this, he pointed at a particular model on the wall that had caught his eye. Daniel and Luke had done a lot of homework on the subject of their intended expansion, and knew more or less what they were looking for, as well as how much they needed to spend on certain-sized boats in order to make it viable. "Of course, the quality and price would determine our interest." he commented.

"Yes, of course, of course," Lim acknowledged, smiling. "Prices I can give you a rough idea of, but quality you will have to take our word for. You can talk to my partner Han about that."

"OK. Can you give me a rough idea in US dollars of the FOB and CIF Southampton prices on that model there?"

"What size do you want?"

"Do you make an eighteen-foot version?"

Lim looked at the brochure he had been holding for the last 15 minutes and opened it to the relevant page for the model concerned.

"Yes, we make an eighteen-footer."

He proceeded to quote a price in US dollars which seemed to Daniel to be extremely low, although Lim was apparently a little confused at this point as to the difference between FOB and CIF pricing, which left Daniel feeling a little concerned. Sensing Daniel's unease, Lim hastily dismissed the misunderstanding by saying that he did not normally deal with any of that side of the business, as Han handled it all in Europe.

"OK" said Daniel. "Do you have a brochure and specification sheet I could show my partner to discuss the possibility of taking things a stage further?"

"Sure," said Lim. He spoke in Chinese to the secretary, who fetched a glossy brochure from the room in the corner and handed it to Daniel.

He flicked through the pages until he found the range he was looking at.

"Are there no full specifications?" he asked, bemused. No boat lengths were shown at all, so why had Edward Lim looked at the brochure for confirmation on the eighteen-footer?

"The specifications have recently changed, so they are on a separate insert." explained Lim. "They're being sent from the factory in the next day or so."

"Could you get one to me as soon as you have it? The specifications and construction data are vital for us to give the boats serious consideration."

"Of course, I will get them to you. I am sorry I'm not more organised, but I don't have everything to hand here in Singapore."

"It's OK, I fully understand the difficulties of running two offices on opposite sides of the globe."

They shook hands, and Daniel made his way back to Beach Road. It would not be long before Luke was back from lunch and they could discuss the new options now on the table.

The moment Daniel left, Xu was on the phone to Han. He told him that he needed thorough specifications on all the boats, and he needed them yesterday. Things were not going to be quite as easy without Gordon, who would have taken things on without questioning everything.

CHAPTER 10

Luke arrived back at the office at about four o'clock, having obviously had a good—and boozy—lunch. Daniel could tell by the look on his face that not much was going to get done that afternoon. They sat and talked for a couple of hours, during which time Daniel commented on the surprising omissions in Lim's knowledge of boats.

Luke pointed out that perhaps, as with so many of these companies, Lim was simply the moneyman with a controlling interest. They both agreed that they would need to get the bulk of the information necessary from his European connection, Han.

The next scheduled trip to the UK was booked for late December, ready for Christmas, and immediately after the New Year, the London Boat Show.

They loosely discussed the possibility of Daniel going to see the factory in Turkey, with Luke going to meet the US company they were interested in.

"You could make a holiday of it in the US and take Michelle with you," Daniel suggested. He knew this would be a good move for both of them and certainly a hit with

Michelle. They agreed to leave that as the loose arrangement until they had more information to hand.

At 6.15pm, Daniel announced that he had to make a move because they were going to Jumbo Seafood on the East Coast Parkway that evening. "In fact, why don't you and Michelle join us, if you're not doing anything? Linda would love you to." he said.

"That sounds great. I'm not that hungry but the thought of those prawns is making my mouth water, and we'll have to eat *something* this evening."

"See you there at 8.30?"

"I'll just phone Michelle and check, but I'm sure she'll want to."

Daniel hung on while Luke phoned home, and when Luke gave him the thumbs up mouthed 'see you later' and left.

***

Daniel arrived home just in time to have a quick swim with Sam and Linda before Sam's bedtime. It was always a treat when Daniel read him his bedtime story, and tonight was no exception. The same episode of Thomas the Tank Engine had to be read not once, but twice. By halfway through the second reading, despite his determined efforts to resist, Sam finally fell asleep.

When Linda and Daniel had showered and changed, Linda went out to fetch Salvia and tell her they were off.

Salvia was in tears, having had yet another bust-up with her boyfriend, but assured them she was OK and that she would go into the main house and watch television until they returned. Daniel made it clear to her that Salim was not welcome in the house, as they had discussed before.

CHAPTER 11

Dorking, England

Maureen Marsh got up at 5.30 that morning, as she had done for years. She drove to the car park on the hill of the North Downs with Toby, her black Labrador, at about 7am, as was her daily routine. As she approached the car park, she felt unusually uneasy. A blue Jaguar was parked in the corner, nose towards her. The windows were misted, and a plume of steam funnelled upwards into the morning air from the back of the car—the engine was obviously running. At first, she assumed a couple were having a passionate time behind the steamy glass. This was unusual; in all the years she had been coming to this particular spot she had not encountered such a thing at this time of day before. She knew it happened during the dark evening hours, particularly at the weekends, but not at seven in the morning.

Deciding to leave them to it, she opened the tailgate and let Toby out. He had his usual excited skittish bluster around the car as Maureen got the lead out and locked the car, but before she could get it on, he darted off towards the

Jaguar. As he approached, he started barking. Maureen ran after him, calling him quietly in case the occupants appeared.

Toby darted around the back of the Jaguar, still making a lot of noise, and Maureen followed. It was only when she got around the back of the car that she noticed that the plume of steam came not from the exhaust pipe but a length of pipe attached it which trailed round and was jammed in the far side window.

The reality of what she was witnessing suddenly hit her. She felt adrenalin hit her bloodstream, and darted around to pull the pipe out of the window. She tried jimmying the doors, but all were locked. Looking around for a tool, she spotted some small rocks lining the edge of the car park perimeter, and gathered the largest she could find. On getting back to the Jaguar, she peered into the small opening where the pipe had been inserted. Seeing nobody on the back seat, she hurled the rock at the back window. The window erupted with a loud crack, and a huge cloud of steam rose from the car.

Maureen put her head in through the window to unlock the door, but as she did so, she nearly passed out from the appalling smell that assaulted her. She fumbled, but managed, letting more air in. When she saw the body slumped over the steering wheel, she turned and was promptly sick.

Toby, seeing her distress, came up to comfort her. Maureen shakily walked back to her car, pulled her mobile phone from the glove compartment, and dialled 999.

The police took about ten minutes to get there, seal off the area, and go to work. It looked like a suicide; the driver, who they had identified from a license in a wallet close to the body, had gassed himself. There had been rain the previous evening, and Gordon had obviously arrived after it as his tyre tracks showed in the sandy ground. There was also a second set of tyre impressions, perhaps belonging to someone who had thought, like Maureen, that the Jaguar was a passion wagon for the evening and departed without looking more closely.

CHAPTER 12

Singapore

As Daniel and Linda drove towards the restaurant complex, the coast was full of people lighting barbecues on the purpose-built grills. They drove on, seeking a parking spot.

"I see Luke and Michelle are already here," Daniel muttered as they passed Luke's car in the car park. They parked a little further on and walked the short distance to the restaurant. The temperature was wonderful, warm and balmy with a light breeze.

"I love it here." Linda commented as they walked arm in arm down the palm-lined walkway and neared Jumbo. "I can't wait for that black pepper crab."

"How did I know you were going for that?"

Luke and Michelle were already seated at one of the round tables outside. There was an air-conditioned section inside, but unless it was raining, they all preferred to eat in the open. As they sat down, Luke immediately picked up the pitcher of beer that was in the centre of the table and poured one each for Linda and Daniel.

"Have you ordered yet?" Daniel asked.

"No we were waiting for you," Michelle smiled.

"Sorry we're a few minutes late. Salvia got another going over from that wretched boyfriend of hers," Linda told them both.

"Bad?" asked Michelle.

"Yes, she was in a bit of a state, but she insists he loves her."

Daniel turned to Luke. "It's when she's alone looking after Sam that it really worries me; I have told her he's banned from the house, but it looks like I'm going to have to lay the law down yet again. I can't say I'm particularly looking forward to it."

"Do you want us to come back with you in case he creates?"

"No. Thanks for the offer, but I'm not even sure when he'll next be there. I think it'll be all right."

They all looked over their menus, although they knew more or less what they were going to order before they arrived. The 'drunken prawns' marinated in wine were a group favourite, as were the black pepper and chilli Sri Lankan crabs.

As they waited, Michelle and Linda continued to chat about the maid situation while Daniel and Luke discussed a Malaysian company they had been advised to buy stocks in. The shares had dropped the moment they had written the cheque out, but they were both convinced that they would bounce back in the near future, and both of them could do with the money as soon as possible. They had product investments to think about, as well as all the marketing they were going to need.

The Chinese tea was poured, the black pepper crab placed on the table, and they all started to tuck in. They were listening avidly to a particularly good-humoured story from Michelle with fingers full of crab when Daniel's mobile started to ring from the depths of his trouser pocket.

"Oh goodness, that's probably Salvia," Linda said, a slight trace of alarm in her voice. They all fell silent with worry as Daniel wiped his hands on a scented towel and dug into his pocket for the phone. He looked at the screen, but no ID showed. With a frown, he flicked it open and put it to his ear.

"Hello?"

"Hi, Daniel?"

"Yes."

"It's Louise. I'm sorry to disturb you at this hour, but I am afraid I have some bad news."

"Bad news, what do you mean?"

The others had all stopped eating now, and were entirely focused on Daniel.

"There's no easy way to tell you this, but I'm afraid that Gordon was found dead in his car this morning with the engine running, a hose plugged in the back of the car and an empty bottle of scotch in his lap."

"Oh my God. Suicide?"

"Yes. The police say it was a fairly typical setup and that he had been drinking heavily last night at the Hatch. He apparently left the pub in a right state, then got in his car and drove off. He told the barman he had just been sacked."

"Do the police think that was the motive?"

"They didn't say. He was apparently waiting at the pub for someone who didn't show."

Daniel turned back to the table and mouthed the word 'Gordon', drawing a finger across his throat. The others looked at him in disbelief.

"OK Louise, thank you. I'll call you tomorrow," Daniel said quietly. He flipped the phone closed and looked at Luke, then the others. They all sat in silence for what seemed like an eternity.

Linda was the first to speak.

"What happened?"

"Gordon gassed himself in his car while apparently paralytic. I feel desperately guilty; he was apparently very low the last time he was seen. I'm sure sacking him must have pushed him over the edge."

"Don't talk such rot," Luke interjected. "He was no good, and he had to go. We can't be everyone's guardian angels, and we certainly couldn't have foreseen the consequences of what was a proper business decision any company worth its salt would have made. There were probably many reasons for doing what he did."

"I hear what you're saying, but what do you think others are going to say? Sacked one day, dead the next. I can't help but feel the two are related, particularly as he took the sacking so badly."

"Well don't let it get to you, either of you. You most certainly had nothing to do with it, and any thinking along those lines will be totally counterproductive," Michelle chipped in. "

"Who found him?" asked Linda.

"I don't know, honey, I was too shocked to ask anything further."

They left almost as soon as the last course had been devoured, and Daniel and Linda drove home in silence to share a brandy on the couch. Daniel tossed and turned in bed that night, unable to sleep. Although he had not particularly liked Gordon, he still felt awful about what had happened, and visions of Gordon dead in his car haunted him all night.

CHAPTER 13

A week had elapsed since Xu's meeting with Daniel; a week which Xu had spent putting together attractive specifications for the models of boat Daniel was interested in. The specification sheets were currently at the printers in Holland Village, and Xu was due to pick them up the next day. He phoned Daniel to arrange a meeting without further delay; both he and Han were now desperate to get things moving.

Vera took the call and put it through.

"Hi, Daniel, Edward here, I am sorry to take so long to come back with your details, but I have been very busy."

"Not a problem Edward, there was no breakneck hurry."

"I have the details now, can we meet to discuss them?"

"Yes, when did you have in mind?"

"How about tomorrow evening?"

"Er, I think I'm out to dinner tomorrow evening. How about tonight?"

"Unfortunately, tomorrow evening is the only time I have before my trip back to Europe. What a shame; I really wanted to speak to you about them personally before I left."

"Well, I tell you what," Daniel said slowly, thinking out loud, "perhaps you and your other half could join my wife and I for dinner tomorrow night?"

"I don't want to put you out, but as it's our only option, let's make a social occasion of it. It would be a nice excuse to meet your wife as well."

"OK, I have a table booked at the Elizabethan Grill at Raffles for eight, so how about we all meet at the Long Bar at seven?"

"That sounds very nice. I'll see you then."

Daniel replaced the receiver and thought for a while before he picked up the phone to explain to Linda that they would have more company for their dinner at the Raffles. They had arranged to meet their friends Pierre and Betty at 7.30pm, and Daniel thought that half an hour would be adequate to get the business chat out of the way before the others arrived.

Linda was not impressed when Daniel told her that two complete strangers would be joining them for dinner, but after a short discussion, she understood the reasoning, and had no doubt they would be very pleasant people.

***

The following evening, Daniel and Linda decided to ask one of their neighbour's daughters if she would mind babysitting Sam. They were not convinced that they had seen the last of Salim, and certainly weren't going to take any risks.

As they arrived at the main entrance of the Raffles, one of the valets recognised them instantly, coming towards them with a beaming smile even before they had stopped the car. He opened the driver's door and Linda got out, leaving the keys in the ignition. Once Daniel had joined her, the valet got in, and the car was whisked away to the underground car park.

The Raffles Hotel was an imposing, elegant and indeed magnificent building that had been practically rebuilt only a few years earlier. The old hotel had had a certain charm and character about it, Daniel recalled, albeit a very well-used and casual appearance. The new, although sharing the same façade, was very different. In order to compete with the best hotels, it was now complete with the mod cons that travellers were demanding.

They walked around Palm Court to where the Long Bar was now situated over two floors. It had originally been a bar of immense presence and character just off the main foyer.

As they entered the bar, the hum of the crowd was audible some distance from the doors. Daniel had a quick scout around the first floor, but did not see Edward Lim, so they walked up the spiral central staircase to the second floor, which was a little quieter. Lim waited at the bar with a very attractive lady, and Daniel made the introductions to Linda.

"The pleasure is all mine, Linda, how very nice to meet you." Lim offered a hand.

"Good evening Edward, it's good to meet you too."

"May I introduce you to my better half, Doris?"

"Well at least he recognises who is the better half!" chuckled Daniel as he and Linda shook hands with Doris.

Before they got settled, Lim asked what he could get them to drink.

"Gin and tonic, please," replied Linda.

"Make that two." Daniel added.

They picked up their drinks and wandered to a table near the top of the spiral staircase, crunching empty pistachio husks underfoot as they went. It was the done thing to throw the shells on the floor, and the ground was constantly covered in them.

As they sat down, Lim opened his briefcase and extracted the details of the boats to show Daniel. As he did, he offered his apologies to Linda for having to conduct business that evening.

"Please don't worry," Linda replied, turning to Doris. "Whereabouts on the island do you live?" she inquired.

"I sorry, but not speak Inglis."

"OK, don't worry," Linda said with a smile. *That's a good start,* she thought to herself. *What an evening this is going to be!*

She turned her attention to the discussion between the men.

***

Xu had known Doris for some years now, having used her services as a prostitute in his native China. As she spoke no English, he knew his secret was safe and that she would pass as his other half without a problem or question. He had briefed her as to the nature of the evening, and she was happy to play along—for a fee.

Xu had been down to the shop earlier that day to collect the printed specification sheets for Daniel, who was now studying the figures. As he did so, Xu watched him carefully for any sign of dissatisfaction.

"What type of buoyancy foam is used, is it open or closed cell?"

"I am sorry Daniel, I really do not know. You will have to talk to Han about the details."

"OK. The specs look good on the face of it, the next thing will be to talk to Han about the import logistics, finer details of the construction, and CE certification."

"He is here the week after next, so maybe you can meet then?"

"We're pretty tied up with the other side of the business, and we're going to be with our factories in Hong Kong and China for the next three weeks or so, but there is no real panic at the moment. Luke and I have some serious number crunching to do, as well as comparison with the American boats we are also looking at. We can't afford to take on both franchises."

"But you are interested?" Lim frowned. He was almost letting some frustration show through, Daniel noticed.

"Yes, very much so, but not until after the London Boat Show in January, and we would obviously need to see the product before committing."

" Oh I see...you want to see the boats."

"Well, yes, of course. We would never buy anything without seeing the product first. No offence, but brochures can be deceiving."

The frown disappeared from Lim's face and he started to smile.

"OK, I tell you what. We can send two boats to you in London for when you arrive at Christmas, completely free of charge."

"That's very kind of you, Edward, but we could not possibly accept that at this stage, I need to do some serious talking with Han first. If Han could come and meet us in London during the show, we can talk about the whole situation then."

"I'll arrange it with Han." Lim had suddenly taken on a more sullen tone after Daniel's dismissal of his offer.

At that moment, Pierre and Betty appeared at the top of the spiral staircase. Linda waved, and they wandered over, then Daniel made the introductions. Betty made a beeline for

Daniel and gave him a big kiss. Xu was alarmed to note she appeared to be Singaporean Chinese and could well be able to communicate fluently with Doris.

Daniel caught the eye of a waiter and ordered another round of drinks.

Doris was now sandwiched between Linda and Pierre, with Betty sitting the other side of Linda. Sure enough, Linda explained to Betty that Doris spoke no English, so Betty immediately switched to Mandarin to address her. Linda turned to talk to Pierre, but quickly suggested swapping places with Doris so she could better communicate with Betty.

At that point, Xu realised that things were going to get awkward unless he acted. He stood, announcing that he and Doris would have to go for a dinner appointment.

"I thought you were joining us?" Daniel said with some surprise.

"Only for the drink, I thought? We do not want to gate-crash the meal with your friends." With that, he spoke quietly to Doris, who picked up her handbag and stood up, downing the rest of her champagne as she did so.

"If they have other arrangements, honey, don't make them feel bad about leaving," Linda said to Daniel with an authoritative look that said more than her words.

"Well, Edward, thank you for coming down to bring the spec sheets. I'm sorry you can't stay longer."

"Next time for sure," said Lim. He bid goodbye to Pierre and Betty, took Doris' arm, and left.

"What did I say wrong?" said Pierre, looking puzzled.

"I have no idea," said Daniel, shaking his head. "I thought it was arranged that they would eat with us this evening. Maybe I got the wrong end of the stick somewhere down the line."

"Well, I'm sure it'll be a much more pleasant evening without them," said Linda. "Doris didn't speak a word of English, and we couldn't have put that strain on Betty all night."

"It seems very odd that an international businessman has a partner who doesn't speak English, particularly in Singapore," noted Pierre.

"From my brief discussion with her I would say she was from Mainland China, not Singapore," said Betty.

"Wherever she was from, he at least brought the information I needed, which was kind of him. I'm sure double-booking dinner was just a misunderstanding."

"You say you met him at the club?" Pierre asked.

"Yes, that's right."

"It's funny. While I don't claim to know even a fraction of the people at the club, one does tend to recognise people. I have to say, I have never seen Edward Lim before." As Pierre mused, they finished their drinks and headed to the other side of the hotel for their dinner.

Lim and Doris were soon forgotten as they all proceeded to have a wonderful evening, laughing, joking and putting the world to rights in general. So good was the evening that they all had too much to drink, and ended up leaving the cars at the hotel and getting taxis home.

CHAPTER 14

It was a couple of days later, on Saturday morning, when Daniel next heard from Lim. He phoned the house, explaining he got the number from directory inquiries to apologise for the misunderstanding on Thursday evening, and explain that it was all an embarrassing mistake on his part. He said he had also forgotten to give Daniel one of the sheets pertaining to the build lay-up on the boats, and offered to run it round to the house for him that afternoon. Daniel had agreed, and given him the address and directions.

Linda answered the door to Lim, who said he had left his car parked outside the gates. As she asked him through to the veranda and closed the front door, she noticed a white Mercedes in the drive and thought for a moment that she had seen the car before, but quickly dismissed it. She showed Lim through to the veranda, where Daniel was working on his laptop and Sam was playing with a garage set he had received for his birthday.

"Do join us for a cup of tea," Linda offered.

"I would like that, thank you."

"Have a seat," Daniel offered, gesturing to one of the empty rattan chairs. Lim took a seat and started to apologise for his misunderstanding about the arrangements the other evening. He claimed to have had a roasting from his wife for getting it wrong. Linda came back with the tea as Lim got the missing paperwork from his case and handed it to Daniel, who scribbled something on a notepad beside him.

"The dates we are in London are on here," Daniel told Lim, handing him the page. "If your colleague can see us during the Boat Show that would make good sense, because we leave for the States straight after."

"I'll pass those dates on to Han, he'll be in Singapore next week. Are you certain you won't have time to see him while he's here?"

"I'm sorry, but I leave for China on Tuesday and there really isn't going to be time. London will be the best place, because there may be some valid points our manager raises that need addressing."

Nodding, Lim turned his attention to little Sam and his garage set. Sam was impressed that someone was showing such an interest and started to show off.

"Cute kid you have," Lim said to Linda.

"Thank you, he is our little treasure, although he has his moments, don't you, poppet?"

Sam smiled at his mother and brought a toy car over to Lim for his perusal. After about ten minutes, having finished his cup of tea, Lim rose, telling Daniel that Han would call to arrange the meeting in London. Daniel said that was fine and that he very much hoped they could do business together. He showed Lim to the door and they shook hands. Lim asked Daniel to contact him when he got back from China if he needed to discuss anything further.

As Daniel returned to the veranda, Linda commented, "I am sure I have seen both Lim and his car before, you know."

"Honestly, honey. There must be thousands of white Mercs in Singapore, why does that one stand out?"

"I don't know, but it just does. Never mind."

"Perhaps from the club? After all, you spend more time there than the rest of us."

"Hmm, I'm not convinced. Still, it may come to me in time."

Linda poured them both another cup of tea and they sat and played with Sam, enjoying a lazy family afternoon at home.

***

Both Luke and Daniel spent a long day in the office on Monday, speaking to customers and sorting out what they needed for their forthcoming trip. Strict instructions were left with Vera to contact them on their mobiles while away if there was anything she couldn't handle, although they knew from past experience that this was unlikely. In reality, the office probably ran more efficiently they weren't there. Once the initial contracts had been set up and the product lines for the various customers were in production, the everyday running was more or less an administrative operation, which Vera was better at than either of them.

CHAPTER 15

The trip to China was a success. Luke and Daniel sorted out production with the factories, and their meetings in Hong Kong had gone equally well. Once back in Singapore, there were only four weeks to catch up on everything before it was time to depart to London for the Christmas holidays. Despite the upheaval, they were quite excited at the prospect of Christmas with all their relatives in the UK, particularly as Sam's own excitement was growing daily.

A few days before they left for the UK, Lim phoned the office. He wanted to confirm that Han would be meeting them on the Monday of the Boat Show, and that they had discussed the supply of a couple of sample boats free of charge if they wished. Luke thanked him for his call and said he looked forward to tying up the deal on their return.

Two days before their departure, Skipper saw the suitcases appear and somehow sensed that this was not just Daniel alone going away on another trip. As the suitcases filled, he realised that everyone was off and he would not be going. He went into a sulk, lying in the kitchen and barely lifting his head to acknowledge anyone. On the evening they finally left the house, he went obediently to the front door, where Linda gave him a big kiss on the cheek and told him that Salvia would be looking after him for a few weeks. As if he understood every word, but did not approve in the least, Skipper turned around, looking very forlorn, and slunk off back to the kitchen.

Daniel, Linda, Sam, Luke, and Michelle were all flying back to Heathrow together, and they met up at Changi Airport. Although Daniel and Luke did a lot of flying, there was a sense of excitement between them about this trip and having their families there.

***

Flight SQ21 was delayed for an hour and a half before take off, but apart from that, the flight was faultless, except that Sam was overtired, irritable, and tearful even before boarding the flight, but still refused to sleep. In the end, Luke had crayoned a colouring book with him until he had eventually dozed off with his thumb in his mouth, much to the relief of the whole party.

Unfortunately, it was only about seven hours before Sam started to awaken, as his tummy told him it was approaching his breakfast time back at home. He woke Linda, and she switched on Sam's TV screen and hoped that the cartoons on the children's channel would capture his imagination, which luckily they did.

Coming in to land at Heathrow, they had had to stack in a circular queuing system for half an hour before landing. It was the beginning of a glorious day over London without a cloud in the sky. As dawn broke, the view below was spectacular, with the ground white with frost and the magnificent spectacle of Windsor Castle standing proudly below them.

They planned to travel to Daniel and Linda's house in Sussex, and had rented a VW Sharan to get down there. They chose to keep the rental car for the duration of their stay—although Daniel and Linda had a car in the UK, Michelle and Luke did not, so they would use this for their independent transport.

It took them about a week to get over the jet lag, but on the third day back, Daniel and Luke spent a full day in the office working with the staff to get the Boat Show organised. They did not have much time, although having done the show for many years; they were well clued up on what was needed. As they worked, Daniel and Luke were told every detail of what had happened to Gordon, with many variations as to why he had done it.

***

Christmas and New Year went as quickly as they had come, but all agreed that it had been one of the more memorable festive seasons. They had all spent the break at Daniel's parents' home in Dorset, which was large enough to swallow them all with ease. It was the most delightful setting for Christmas, with the house's blazing log fires and beamed ceilings adding to the atmosphere. They all delighted in roasting chestnuts in the evenings, and became thoroughly relaxed.

Linda had phoned Salvia on Boxing Day to ensure all was well, and was assured that things were fine. She had also called their neighbours, partly to wish them a Happy Christmas, and partly to check out Salvia's story, which proved to be only partially true, but they were quick to reassure her that Skipper was fine, everything was under control, and there was nothing to worry about.

The office was closed for the entire Christmas and New Year period, and did not open again until the third of January. Luckily, Luke and Daniel were confident they were ready to go and set up the London Boat Show stand on the fourth, fifth, and sixth.

CHAPTER 16

Earls Court, London

When the fourth of January came, Daniel and Luke were thrown back in at the deep end. No matter how organised they had thought they were, there were the usual last-minute panics for things that had been forgotten, and increasingly frayed tempers. They found themselves still drilling and screwing things together even after the exhibition centre staff had announced that the doors were being locked and all exhibitors and contractors should leave the building. They finally had everything complete by nine o'clock on the evening of the sixth, and drove back to Sussex exhausted. They had given strict instructions for Louise and the sales staff to be there by 8.30 on opening day, telling them that both Daniel and Luke would be in by about midday with their families in tow.

***

The opening day was press and VIP day. The staff had all spent most of the morning finalising the stand, polishing the boats, making sure the prices were with all the brochures, and generally titivating things. When Daniel, Luke, and their families arrived, the stand looked superb. They congratulated everyone for their efforts, even though they both felt that most of the effort had come from them. Luke broke open the first bottle of Lanson, and they all toasted to having a good show. The champagne flowed freely on that first day, with every existing customer, press representative, and potential customer offered a glass. It was a good kick-off to the show.

While the staff stayed in hotels close to the exhibition centre, Daniel and Luke were commuting daily, making the most of the break from Singapore with their wives. Linda drove them all home that first evening, as she had refrained from drinking.

The weekend at the show was exactly as expected, a complete deluge of the general public and their children— some of whom were extremely unruly and badly behaved. Everyone on the stand had at least one run in with a parent who felt that their child had a given right to crawl all over the boats, scratching the decks with their hard shoes and spilling Coke and ice cream over them. Luke had amused them all on the Sunday when a particularly obnoxious father, who could not string a sentence together without an expletive between each word, had argued about his child not being allowed on a particular boat. Luke had reached the end of his tether and told him to piss off.

They were all looking forward to Monday; it was quieter, but generally visited by a better percentage of serious buyers.

CHAPTER 17

Earls Court, London Boat Show

At about 11am on Monday morning, Daniel and one of the female staff were on the stand. Luke had not come in that day, as he and Michelle had gone to visit some of her relations in Bedford.

Once the stand was empty, Daniel saw a man of Middle Eastern appearance approach, and wondered if it was Han, a fact that was soon confirmed when he came up to the stand. He was accompanied a by a tall dark-haired woman who was dressed to the nines. At first glance, Daniel thought she was about to appear on stage at a nightclub—how thoroughly out of place she looked! Han left her standing by one of the boats as he introduced himself.

"Good to meet you," Daniel remarked. "Mr Lim tells me you are the man with all the answers."

Han smiled and replied in strongly accented English, "Yes, I am in charge of production and European operations. Lim has very little to do with it really. I am very pleased to meet you."

"Let's go and have a seat," said Daniel, ushering Han to the seating area. Lim had obviously informed Han of the models that were of interest to Daniel, as he was armed with the relevant brochure as well as one for a range of larger sports boats.

As they settled opposite each other, Daniel started to try and size Han up. He was very expensively dressed in a smart suit covered by a Mohair knee-length coat and wore a gold Rolex on his wrist. He was probably about 35 or 36, with hair that appeared to be thinning on top, but was nevertheless fit and good-looking. Daniel imagined he was probably quite a hit with the ladies, although judging by the one he had brought to the stand, not necessarily the right types.

As they started to talk, interruptions began to happen in their droves. Progress was slow, and after about 20 minutes and many apologies, Daniel suggested that they meet after the show had closed that evening.

"Which hotel are you staying at?" he asked.

"One a little far from here," came the response.

"Well, do you want me to meet you at your hotel?" Daniel offered.

"Not necessary, we can meet around here somewhere."

"Well OK, how about the Gloucester Hotel on Gloucester Road? It's only round the corner. We can meet in the bar at about seven?"

"That will be fine. Where is this hotel?"

Daniel spent the next couple of minutes drawing a map on the back of a flyer for Han. He handed it to him as yet another customer interrupted, requiring more information on any discount he might offer in lieu of a part-exchange. Han handed Daniel a card, shook his hand, said he would see him later, and wandered off. Daniel put the card straight into his pocket and concentrated his attention on the customer in front of him. The rest of the day seemed fairly hectic, and was certainly busier than he had remembered the Mondays of previous years to be. He was pleased that Luke would be on hand to help again tomorrow.

***

At about 5.30, things began to quieten down a bit, and one of Daniel's friends wandered to the stand. The three members of staff were easily going to be able to cope for 15 minutes, so Daniel and Mike decided to go to the Guinness stand for a swift half before the close of the show. It wasn't until Daniel started to tell Mike about his forthcoming meeting that he remembered Han's card and extracted it from his pocket. He looked at it, puzzled. It showed an address in Israel, and there was no mention of the Singapore or Istanbul addresses. After some discussion, they both drew the conclusion that the card must have been for another venture Han was involved with and he had handed it over by mistake.

Daniel left at 6.40pm and went to collect his car. His trusted BMW 635 had been in the family for many years and had become part of the furniture. It was getting on, but still looked good, was exceptionally comfortable, and went faultlessly. It was ideal to keep locked in the garage for visits back to the UK.

The drive to the Gloucester took ten minutes—twice as long it would have taken to walk, but the traffic was appalling that particular evening. He was about to turn into the underground car park when the doorman ushered him into a space right outside the front doors of the hotel. He duly parked and thanked the doorman, then entered the hotel and walked into the bar, immediately spotting Han sitting at a table in the corner.

Having sorted out drinks, they made polite small talk. After a few minutes, Daniel got a sheet out of his briefcase with a list of questions he had prepared and started to go through them one by one.

"Having looked at the specifications in depth, there are some fundamentals we need assurance of before we can take things any further," he said.

"Of course, I understand," Han said sharply. "But let me tell you about us first. We make many types of boat in all countries, including Germany, Sweden, and America, so we are very good at this job. You must not worry about specifications, all our customers are very happy."

Daniel was annoyed at being told what he should and should not worry about, but let the comment go. He replied as diplomatically as he could.

"Well, with all due respect, we have never done business with your company or come across your products before, so I am afraid we do need assurance that everything meets the legal requirements for the UK, as well as our own standards. I'm sure you can appreciate that. If you supply Germany, that does answer one of my questions, which was whether the boats all conform to the new CE regulations."

"Yes, yes, they meet all regulations. We can send two boats for you to see the quality."

Daniel did not particularly like Han's forceful manner, and was determined to make sure he was happy with everything before committing. He was certainly not going to have two boats forced upon him in this way.

"I appreciate the offer, but to save you the trouble I have spoken with my partner, who is going to the US in a couple of weeks time," he said. "If it is OK, I will visit you in Turkey at the same time to see your factory and look at the product. If all is well, we can finalize things then."

"But it is no trouble for us to send you the boats, you need not waste your time to come to Turkey," Han insisted.

"No, I really would like to. We would not entertain such a venture without visiting the factory first."

Han looked slightly despondent at Daniel not accepting his offer. Daniel briefly thought that perhaps that was the Turkish way, and that he had somehow offended him, but he really did not care. He had to be sure.

"You will have to let me come back to you on that; I am not sure I am in Turkey then, and I may have to change arrangements," said Han.

"OK, let me know and we'll arrange dates shortly, but in the meantime, assuming that it all goes ahead, on what terms do you normally do business? I assume you want telegraphic transfer of the funds before shipment, but what guarantees can you give us to the UK rights for the products? Do you have a dealer agreement I could look at?"

"We will supply the models you want, and then split the profit when you sell them. Later on, we will also want to set up a London showroom. We will pay for it."

Daniel looked at Han quizzically for a moment. It appeared that what they really wanted was a joint venture, which was not of the least interest to Daniel and Luke. As for a London showroom, Daniel was almost lost for words.

"A London showroom? That's an unusual way of thinking, and would certainly not come cheap. I must say, I'm not sure how effective it would be either, unless it was on the Thames. Even then, it's very extravagant, and the company would have to be making serious money to support such a luxury. I can't say we would necessarily want to be involved, if that's your thinking."

Han realised he would have to back off a little. His idea that this show of monetary power would impress Daniel had backfired. "Never mind; I was thinking that it was a good idea, but you must know better, and we certainly want to work with you."

They continued chatting for about 15 minutes, but got nowhere, with Han insisting that he would retain ownership of the boats until they were sold, and then the profit would be split equally in two. This was an odd way to conduct business to Daniel; he had never come across such an idea from a manufacturer before. Most manufacturers were normally clamouring for money even before the craft were built, and there were numerous complications with operating the business in the way Han wanted, if indeed it was workable.

Daniel thought about how they would cope with demonstration boats, on which there would probably be an initial loss. Who was responsible for import duties and shipping? Who would finance engines and trailers? Who shouldered the potential loss from any over allowance on a part-exchange? Which half of the profit would foot the bill for all the show and marketing costs? The questions in Daniel's head were numerous, but it was clear that Han was simply not interested in the detail.

In the end, Daniel decided that the best thing to do would be to see the boats. If they were indeed as good as they were promised to be, these points would be worth arguing. He concluded that it was most likely just the Turkish way, and that Han was trying to be generous, but he could not dislodge the uneasy feeling in his gut. He asked Han for the second time that day where he was staying.

"I am staying near Baker Street."

"I can give you a lift back if you like. I need to get on to the M40, so it's no trouble."

Han looked a little uneasy, but accepted the offer.

Daniel got up. "I'm just going to the toilet first, I'll be back in a minute."

With that, Han got up too. "I will come with you," he said.

"Er, OK," said Daniel. "We'd better take our coats and briefcases then, we can't leave them unattended."

Han followed Daniel to the toilets in the foyer, and stood at the next urinal, although the rest of them were free. Daniel hated people crowding him, so he turned around and shut himself in one of the cubicles. When he came out, Han was waiting for him by the basins. Daniel washed his hands, and Han followed him back through the foyer and out to the car.

When they got outside, Daniel tipped the doorman and ushered Han to his BMW.

Han broke into a smile. "You have my car!"

Daniel looked at him. "What do you mean?"

"I have this car at home. I love this car."

"Yes, I'm very happy with mine too."

They spent the 15-minute journey to Baker Street discussing cars, and BMWs in particular. Han said he was having trouble getting hold of certain parts for his car back at home. Daniel was a little confused by this comment, as he knew that all the main dealers could locate parts for this model, but suggested that Han give him a list. Provided they were not too big, he would bring the parts out to when he came out to Istanbul. Han was most grateful for this and said he would fax the details when he got back.

"Where is your hotel from here?" asked Daniel.

"I am staying at a friend's apartment, so please just drop me here."

"Don't worry, I'll take you to the door. It's a miserable evening."

"No, please drop me here. It is not easy to find, and I can walk. It is very close."

Daniel found this most odd. For some reason, Han clearly did not want him to know where he was staying. Perhaps it was a little scruffy and he was embarrassed.

Before Han got out of the car, he turned to Daniel. "I would like to see your premises before I leave; when can I do this?"

This comment caught Daniel a little off guard, as he had been worried about doing things the other way round. "It's going to be difficult during the show this week, but how about next Monday?"

"That will be fine. Where do I find you?"

"Give me your number in London, and I'll phone you for your fax number and send a map through to you."

"I don't know my number, so I will contact your office on Monday."

"Oh, OK," said Daniel. "We'll do it that way then."

Han smiled, they shook hands, and he disappeared down the pavement as Daniel waited to pull out into the traffic.

Daniel spent the first ten minutes of the journey home going over everything that had been said. Despite all the things that didn't seem to fit, he told himself that if he viewed and liked the boats, they could make it work. After all, there was good profit to be made, and from the brochures the boats appeared to be just the market fillers they were looking for. However, the Turks certainly had an unusual way of doing things.

Daniel stopped at a garage to collect a packet of crisps and a sandwich. He was very hungry, and could not wait until he got home, so a snack was going to have to do for dinner tonight. As he pulled off the M40 and onto the M25 southbound, he switched on the radio. It was tuned to Radio 2, something he missed in Singapore, although these days he was rarely alone to listen to it. *I Feel it in My Fingers, I Feel it in My Toes* broke the silence. He cranked up the volume and enjoyed one of his favourite tunes, one that conjured very happy memories for both him and Linda.

When he returned, the others were all in the sitting room in front of a log fire watching the end of the evening news. He poured himself a whisky and sat down. After the news had finished, they exchanged accounts of the day, and he brought them all up to date with the meeting with Han, including his thoughts and misgivings. They all listened attentively.

CHAPTER 18

It was on the Thursday of the show that they next saw Han, or more accurately, the lady who had been with him on the last occasion. Daniel noticed her standing beside one of the adjacent stands as he came back from one of the bars with a load of Coca-Colas. She glanced at him as he walked by, but as he smiled at her, she looked away, apparently embarrassed. He was going to go back and say hello, but when he turned round after placing the drinks on the table, she was gone.

About two hours later, Han arrived at the stand, wanting to know when they could meet at Daniel and Luke's premises. Daniel drew directions for him, suggesting that he come down on Monday and that they go out for lunch at the local pub. He asked him if he had had any thoughts on his trip to Turkey, but Han said it was yet to be confirmed. When Daniel said he had seen his colleague a couple of hours earlier, Han said that was impossible, and that Daniel was mistaken. Daniel knew that this was untrue, but was not going to argue the point, particularly as he did not even know what the relationship between the two of them was.

Han handed Daniel another brochure and indicated that the prices marked were inclusive of shipping to the UK, with the freight being organised at the Istanbul end. Daniel was surprised at how low the prices were, and could not help but think how casual it all was; figures jotted with biro on a brochure. Still, it was what the jottings said that mattered.

Han handed Daniel another business card, this time with a mobile number on it, and suggested he ring him on that number if he had any questions. It was a different card from the first one he had received, and indeed carried an Istanbul address. The stand was by this time busy, and all of them were flat out, so Han was soon on his way.

***

Xu had arrived in London the previous morning, and that evening he and Han spent several hours trying to think of the best way to ensure that Daniel was given the right impression when he went to see the factory. It was no longer a case of if, but when. Sooner was better from their point of view, so that they could get the business underway.

They had discussed the prices of the boats Daniel had requested and decided to subsidise the shipping cost considerably in order to make the deal tantalisingly attractive to Daniel and Luke, who despite all the assurances under the sun were not going to simply fall hook line and sinker as they had hoped. Again they cursed the Gordon's stupidity. With him, they would have only needed to send the first two samples, rather than needing to worry about scrutiny.

Xu was on the midday flight to Istanbul the following day. He was going to get things sorted out with the factory, and would ring Han on Monday, after the final meeting with Daniel.

***

The last day of the show was always busy, but the quality of the customers tailed off after lunch, as the bargain hunters came round looking for anything on sale 'cheap'. Daniel and Luke had never subscribed to the idea of selling off certain items of stock cheaply on the last day to a bunch of vultures that came specifically for that reason. They had always maintained that their goods were fairly priced from the word go, so why should someone there on the last day pay anything less than people who came on the first day?

They spent the last couple of hours before the show finished looking through the order sheets. They had been keeping a rough tally as the days had drifted by, but now was crunch time. After collating them, Luke and Daniel were pleased to discover it had been a good show for them, and if all the orders taken went through to completion, they could be very comfortable. The figures showed a one-third increase on the previous year.

They packed up everything that could be easily stolen that evening, leaving the bulk of the stand and all the large boats to be taken away during the next couple of days. However, it was still after 9pm before they made it out of the exhibition hall that night, and they stopped for a Burger King on North End Road on the way home. Linda and Michelle were not expecting them back before 10pm, and would not have cooked. As they ate, they had a post mortem about the show, discussing how they had felt it had gone and what they could do better for the Southampton show in September.

Both men were in bed and asleep within half an hour of arriving home, shattered from the week's events.

CHAPTER 19

The next morning, the first person in the household to wake up was Sam, as usual. Luke was going to go back to Earls Court to oversee the dismantling of the stand, while Daniel was going into the office, primarily to meet Han and introduce him to everyone.

When Daniel arrived in the office at nine o'clock that morning, he called Vera in Singapore to see if all was well. It was; one of the large deals they had been working on for later that season had just come to fruition in the form of a confirmed order. Daniel asked Vera to fax it to him at the UK office, and was cheered immeasurably, phoning Luke on his mobile to break the good news.

Han arrived at the office at 12.15 in a Ford Focus, accompanied by a lady he introduced as Maya, his wife. She was about 5'7" with shoulder length natural blond hair and beautiful pale blue eyes. Daniel immediately liked her, and he could not help wondering what on earth Han had been doing with the other woman at the show.

Thinking of the presence of Maya at lunch, Daniel quickly phoned Linda to see if she could join them. She immediately agreed. While they waited for her to arrive,

Louise made them all a coffee and Daniel introduced them to the remainder of the office staff. They then moved out to the workshop, and Daniel showed them around the warehouse.

Linda arrived just as they finished the tour. They all hopped into the Sharan and went down to the Dog & Duck for a hot pub lunch. Han departed to the bar while Linda fetched the menus.

When they were settled at a table, Han announced that neither he nor Maya would be eating anything because of Ramadan. Surprised, Daniel shot a glance in Linda's direction.

"That's a shame, the food here is excellent," she said. "You don't mind if we order?"

"No, please carry on," said Maya. "Han should have let you know we could not eat at lunchtime, I am sorry." She glared at her husband.

Linda took to Maya immediately after that, and they were soon chatting like long lost friends. Maya spoke word-perfect English with very little accent, and was apparently a senior nurse at one of the main hospitals in Istanbul. Daniel and Linda agreed she must be a brilliant nurse with her naturally calming way.

Han, on the other hand, seemed quite agitated throughout the whole meeting, trying to keep Maya from chatting and eager to drag the conversation back to what he wanted to talk about.

Daniel and Linda's food arrived and they started to tuck in as Han and Maya watched. Linda, sensing an atmosphere between the other two, managed to involve them both in light conversation, and soon the mood had lifted. They all ended up having a good time, with even Han telling some jokes.

Before they left the pub, Daniel asked Han if he had decided which parts he wanted for his car. Han said he could do with a driver's-side window, because his had been smashed when his car was robbed. Daniel said he could order one for him, but it would have to be sent out by courier.

"Thank you, Daniel," said Han. "Please fax a price to my number in Istanbul including carriage, and I will let you know."

They all left the pub feeling comfortable in each other's company, and returned to the office. Linda left straight after dropping them off, telling Maya to keep in touch, while Maya and Han got into the Focus and Daniel waved them off.

Daniel spent what remained of the afternoon in the office. At about 5pm, he got into the BMW and headed home. Luke finally arrived back at the house at about 7.30 that night, pleased to be able to report that everything at the show was now clear and they would not have to go back the following day as they had done in previous years.

Michelle, Linda, and Sam were due to fly back to Singapore the following evening, so Daniel and Luke got out of their hair that morning, but arrived home at lunchtime to spend the afternoon with them before they departed.

Luke was due to go to the States the following Monday, initially to a trade fair, then on to the boat factory. Daniel planned to travel to Istanbul three days after that, on the Thursday. They would then both head back to London, and ultimately on to Singapore together.

They headed up to the airport that evening in the two cars. Daniel and Luke took the rental back, having dropped off the girls to check in and put the BMW in the multi-storey. They then headed back to meet them in the McDonalds in Terminal 3 departure area. For Luke and Daniel, this would be their only meal this evening.

At passport control, they all said their goodbyes. Subdued, Daniel and Luke waved their families off and headed home. They both collapsed in front of the late evening news and enjoyed the peace and quiet before Daniel retired for an early night, leaving Luke watching a late-night western.

CHAPTER 20

Daniel and Luke spent the next few days finalising their requirements from the US boat company and what Luke needed to discuss with them, as well as exactly what Daniel needed to look for in Turkey. They both agreed that things seemed much more straightforward with the US company—indeed, they had already sent over certification forms—but resolved not to decide which company they would go with until they had made their visits. After all, the Turkish manufacturer was definitely better value for money, even if the process was going to be more difficult to administer.

That Friday, Han rang to confirm that he could be in Istanbul for the end of the following week, and asked Daniel to let him know his confirmed flight dates. Daniel passed them on, mentioning he had also obtained details for replacing the window glass of the BMW, but needed to know the chassis number. Han said he would fax it over.

They drove to Daniel's parents that weekend to unwind, heading back on the Sunday evening to give Luke a chance to pack. Daniel took Luke to catch his flight to Newark at eight. Afterwards, he headed for the office, but the amount of traffic he encountered on the M25 meant the journey that had taken half an hour in one direction took just over two hours in the other. When he eventually arrived, he phoned Han to advise him that he would be arriving at Istanbul airport at 2.10pm on Thursday. He planned to stay until the Sunday, when he would fly back to London on the 1.30pm flight.

Daniel had checked the prices of hotels in Istanbul and was advised that he could get a reasonable three-star with en-suite facilities for about £45 per night. He knew he only had about £700 credit left on his Barclaycard, and did not want to appear a pauper, but there was no necessity to spend too much. The simple fact was, he couldn't.

"Could you please book me into a three-star hotel not too far from the city centre?" he asked Han. "It doesn't need to be too grand, as long as it's clean and has an en-suite bathroom."

"Do not worry about the hotel, I will sort it for you," Han responded.

"Thank you. I know the Holiday Inn is good value, so perhaps you could look at availability there first? By the way, I still haven't received the chassis number to order your window."

"I'm sorry, I have been busy."

"Don't apologise, it's not me driving around without one. It's up to you, but if you get me what they need I'm happy to order the part for you."

"OK. Thank you, I will see you Thursday."

Daniel put the phone down and was quickly whisked away to spend the rest of the day in meetings with the sales manager, discussing how best to follow up on all the leads from the show.

CHAPTER 21

As Luke checked in, he was pleased to find that he had been upgraded from economy to business class. In such comfort, the seven-hour flight from Heathrow to Newark seemed to take half that time, and before he knew it he was on a hotel bus heading for a Best Western in Manhattan. He and Daniel had both agreed to keep the costs to a minimum, as his wallet was suffering.

Later that afternoon, Luke found himself wrapped up against the bitter New York winter making the 35-minute walk to the Javits Center, where he would spend the afternoon. He was there to look for new ideas, products, and manufacturers for their leisure business. Luke was methodical and thorough, and if there were anything there worth looking at, he would find it.

Luke spent a couple of hours circling the show before returning to his hotel, via a Burger King, to have a shower and get a good night's sleep. He was going to return to spend Tuesday at the show before heading off on his Wednesday morning flight to Florida.

He was up early on the Wednesday morning, and wandered to a breakfast bar he had seen on West 57th Street for a big American breakfast, which set him up well for the day. He left Newark later that morning, and arrived at Jacksonville Airport by late afternoon, taking a short bus ride to the Alamo car rental centre, where he had a car booked. The centre was out of compacts of the type Luke had booked, so they gave him a mid-size Pontiac Bonneville for the same price. The car was brand new, with only 12 miles on the clock. Luke was beginning to enjoy this trip.

Luke made the three-hour journey northwest to the town of Waycross in Georgia that evening, where he found a Days Inn and settled for the evening. He phoned the office back in the UK, which was 5 hours ahead, and gave the hotel number to Louise to pass onto Daniel to phone him back. Many years before, Daniel and Luke had found using the hotel phone a little too convenient for quick conversations and had been bowled over by the size of the bills they had been presented with on check out, but now they knew better.

The next morning, he headed off to see the US boat factory. Bob, their export manager, greeted him and gave him a detailed tour of the plant. The factory must have covered an acre of ground, with a further two or three of storage outside, and had boats at all stages of construction. There were dozens of people working in every section of the production line, all dressed in white overalls, with dust masks where necessary. It was an impressive place—as indeed it had to be to produce 4000 boats a year. Luke guessed that Daniel would find a similar scene in Turkey given that the quoted production from the two factories was so similar, although he somehow doubted the working practice would be quite so tidy, organised, or up to date.

After the tour, Luke was shown the new products due to be launched, and as if he were not impressed enough already, this tipped the balance. They should be tying in with a company that was moving forward as aggressively as this one, and they could not have wished for nicer, more genuine, or more hospitable people to deal with. Both men liked the Americans' openness and warmth, and had always felt at home there.

Heading back to the motel that afternoon after having been treated to a fabulous buffet lunch by his hosts, Luke thought hard about calling Daniel's trip off, but realised that his tickets and hotel would already be booked.

Not to worry, he thought to himself, *we can compare notes when we get back to London.*

CHAPTER 22

Daniel was booked on an early-morning British Airways flight from Heathrow and had ordered a taxi to collect him from the house at 5am. Before leaving, he phoned home and had a chat with Linda to establish everything was fine. He promised to call her again on his return to London on Sunday.

As Daniel examined the departure lounge screen to see his boarding time, a wave of uncertainty came over him. It dawned that he was heading out to Turkey without knowing where he was staying, the location of the factory he was supposed to be visiting, or even very much about his hosts. He tried to push the feeling away, telling himself it was just a standard business trip like those he had taken many times in the past.

He moved to a few vacant seats grouped together and sat in the middle of them, putting his briefcase on the seat next to him. As he sat down, he heard a sharp crack from the pocket of his coat and swiftly stood again to see what had made the noise. It was his mobile phone, which now had a large crack down one side and would not power on.

"Bloody typical!" Daniel muttered, cross at his own carelessness. He sat down again and started to read the *Telegraph* he had bought in the terminal.

He soon found himself looking blankly at the page as his mind wandered. Niggling doubts came over him as he recounted to himself the details of the meeting with Han at the Gloucester Hotel. He remembered that they had never really discussed the true course or operation of the business, along with how flippantly the monetary aspect of it had been dismissed. He attempted to reassure himself once again that this was obviously their way of doing business, but the more he thought about it, the more ill at ease he became. Before he could ponder further, Daniel noticed that his flight status had changed to 'Boarding', so he got up and started to wander slowly towards the gate.

As soon as he got to his seat, he pulled out the complimentary in-flight magazine, turned to the map in the centre, and studied it to see exactly where Istanbul was. He had never researched that area in any great detail, but had been slightly surprised when Han had advised him to bring some warm clothes because it was currently colder than London. The seat belt signs went off briefly once they had levelled out from take off, but they soon lit again, staying on for one of the most turbulent flights Daniel had experienced in a long time.

As the plane cut though the air, he wondered how Luke had got on at the factory in the US, and looked at his watch to try to work out if he had finished there. Daniel was itching to know things had gone.

On touchdown, he got off the aircraft and followed the flow of people through to Immigration, where he joined one of the queues and shuffled forward patiently with everyone else. As he looked around, he noticed that all the security officers were armed, and there were a lot of them. He was also aware of how long it was taking to stamp every person through. When he finally got to the front of the queue, he handed his passport over the counter, only to have it smartly thrust back at him with the words "Visa, visa!"

With that, the Immigration Officer started to usher the next person forward, but Daniel stood fast. Nobody had mentioned needing a visa.

"What do you mean, visa?" Daniel asked.

"There visa." The officer pointed impatiently.

Daniel followed the direction of his finger and wandered round to a small kiosk alongside the main immigration desks. 'Visa' was written above it, with a series of costs in different currencies below it and another long queue, which Daniel reluctantly joined.

"Great start!" he mumbled.

Once at the front of the queue, he handed over his passport and a £20 note; the smallest denomination he had on him.

"No, *ten* pounds, see?" The man pointed at the sign.

"Yes, I know it is ten pounds. I am giving you twenty, you give me ten back."

"No, ten pounds only."

Daniel's irritation was beginning to show as he thrust the £20 note forward only to have it pushed back at him again. The man who had just been served had been on his flight, and seeing what was happening, turned to Daniel.

"I learned my lesson on last time I came in, it's absurd. I have two tens for your twenty if you like."

"Thanks very much." Daniel took the two tens gratefully, handing one to the cashier and giving the gentleman back a twenty-pound note.

"Have a good trip," the other man said as he headed to the queue for Immigration.

Daniel turned and acknowledged him with a wave. "Thanks again for your help!"

They stamped Daniel's passport with the visa and gave it back to him without a hint of courtesy.

Daniel went back to Immigration and was finally allowed through to luggage reclaim, where his case was one of the few still left on the carousel. Daniel gathered it and wheeled it to Customs, half-expecting to be stopped there as well. To his surprise, he went straight through and into the sea of people waiting to meet various flights.

He looked around, but did not see Han in the immediate vicinity, so wandered around for a while looking for him. In the end, with no sign of Han at all, Daniel stood against one of the pillars close to the main exit and kept an eye out for him.

After about half an hour, he began to become slightly anxious, and started to wonder whether Han had ever had any intention of meeting him there. Maybe he had missed a message asking him to get a cab to a certain hotel? He realised that he could not even phone Han to check, because the number was stored in his broken mobile phone.

The bad flight, airport queues, and visa drama had added up to make Daniel feel quite uneasy, and with nobody to meet him, he was beginning to feel bad-tempered and fed up. He decided to give it another half-hour before he made his own way to a hotel.

CHAPTER 23

Istanbul

It was with more than a small sense of relief that Daniel noticed Han walking through the main doors, heading towards the meeting area. As Han saw him, he smiled, and begun to apologise before they were within 15 feet of each other.

"Have you waited a long time?" asked Han.

In the British tradition, Daniel responded, "No, no, not long at all."

"I was unavoidably delayed at the office, and I could not ring you to let you know."

"Don't worry. You're here now, that's the main thing."

"Let me take your case, my car is not far."

Daniel followed Han outside. The air was cold, but it was a beautifully sunny day. Daniel loved this type of weather, cold but clear and crisp.

"Was your flight from London good?" Han enquired as they made their way through the car park.

"I would like to say yes, but it was a little bumpy."

Daniel looked out for a BMW, but they came to a halt by the boot of a silver Mercedes Benz 200. Han opened the boot and placed Daniel's case inside it.

"You've got a new car?" Daniel asked as Han shut the boot and went to the driver's side. Daniel got in to the passenger seat.

"No," replied Han. " I have had this car for many years, it is good for business."

How odd, Daniel thought as he looked around the interior of the car. He had not mentioned the Mercedes at all when they had been discussing cars back in London. What was more, there were no personal possessions inside, not even loose change or CDs. The boot had been the same, completely empty. The windows were misted up on the inside, and it felt damp, as if the upholstery had been recently washed. He would have said it was a rental car, but here Han was, claiming it to be his. The whole affair struck Daniel as being very strange, but perhaps it would all make sense in time.

"Nice," he said, hiding his concerns. "I hope you didn't go to the trouble of cleaning it all for my benefit."

"It was a good excuse; it needed a clean anyway."

The Merc E200 was an automatic and incredibly sluggish, but that didn't stop Han wringing every last drop of power out of it by keeping his foot welded to the floor. As they swung straight into a stream of traffic on the dual carriageway, causing others to brake, Han announced that he had once been a racing driver. It appeared he was determined to prove this to Daniel, who hoped that by engaging him in conversation, he might slow Han down a bit, He had never before felt so uncomfortable as a passenger; in fact, he was plain frightened, and covering up his nerves the best he could.

"Of course, the trouble is on the open road and the idiots you have to look out for," Han was saying. "I'm sure it's the same in England."

Indeed there are idiot drivers, thought Daniel, *and one of them is in the car with me.*

When Han continued at the same furious pace, Daniel asked, "Are we in a hurry?"

"Yes, we have to get to the restaurant for lunch before it closes. We were supposed to be there by now. It's my fault."

After about 20 minutes of their white-knuckle ride, they arrived at a restaurant set into a hill overlooking the Bosphorus. It was virtually empty, with only a handful of diners finishing their lunch. Han and Daniel were ushered to a window seat, where Han ordered for both of them, then began to explain their itinerary for the next couple of days.

"After lunch, I will take you to your hotel, and then this evening we go to a very famous fish restaurant," he said. "Tomorrow we go to the boat factory."

"Where is the boat factory in relation to us?" Daniel inquired. He was feeling a little more comfortable having had a few slurps of Coca Cola, but hoped that the journey the next day would not be quite so breakneck.

"It is about three hours' drive. On Saturday, I will take you for a ride on my boat and we'll see Istanbul from the water. It will give you another view of the city."

Daniel was already fascinated with Istanbul, and was keen to learn as much as he could about it while he was here. He hoped that Han would set aside a few 'unorganised hours' for Daniel to do his own thing and see a little of its history.

They spent the rest of the meal discussing Istanbul; its politics, its building policies, and everything that Han felt was wrong with them. Talk about boats could wait until the factory visit.

Daniel was not particularly hungry, having eaten on the aircraft, but ate as much as possible of what was put in front of him. They eventually left the restaurant at about 4pm, and Han announced that he was going to drop Daniel at his hotel to freshen up before their meal later that evening.

"Do you have much of a social life in Singapore?" Han asked Daniel as they drove.

"Yes, my wife and I have a very enjoyable one. It's a sociable place."

"Istanbul is also sociable. I can assure you that while you are here, you will not sleep!"

Oh, great, thought Daniel sarcastically, *that's just what I need.*

All he had wanted to do was to see the factory and the products, a little of historic Istanbul, and go back to his family. Han, it was beginning to become apparent, had different ideas.

"That's very hospitable of you, but I'm not a great one for night life, I'm afraid, and I need all the sleep I can get after the last couple of months," explained Daniel. "A nice meal and bed in the evenings will do me well."

"A few days without sleep will not harm you," Han insisted.

He's imposing his will on me, and I don't like it, Daniel thought quietly to himself, now worrying about how to get out of it. He suddenly feared that this trip was not going to be what he had thought.

The car was silent for some minutes as they tore up one of the dual carriageways, until Han pointed.

"There is your hotel."

Daniel glanced in the general direction of Han's arm, but could only see a magnificent skyscraper built from reflective glass.

"Where?" said Daniel, sure that he had missed something.

"This one, you must be able to see."

"The big glass one?"

"Yes, this is your hotel."

Daniel looked again, feeling dread churn in his stomach. He only had a little credit left on his Barclaycard.

"We have to do a U-turn to get back to it," Han announced, "It is fantastic, yes?"

"Fantastic it may be, but it's not at all what I asked you to book for me. I really do not want to spend too much, and I bet it's more than forty-five pounds a night."

"Of course, it is the best in Istanbul."

"Han, this really isn't necessary at all. I have just had a very expensive Christmas and New Year, and until I get back to Singapore to top up the finances I don't want to spend too much."

"Do not worry about it, you will enjoy it there!"

Daniel looked out of the passenger window, rolled his eyes and let out a quiet sigh. He was not at all happy; it appeared that Han was not taking a blind bit of notice of his requests.

As they drew up under the canopy for the foyer, the doors of the car were opened for them. Daniel's case was collected from the boot, and he was ushered to reception.

Han did all the talking. In seconds, he had the key and was heading for the lifts. The hotel was very expensively furnished, with polished granite and marble adorning every surface. They stepped out of the lift, and within a few yards had reached Daniel's room. As Daniel followed Han through the door, the porter followed.

Han watched for a reaction from Daniel as they entered the opulent suite. Daniel said nothing, desperately wondering how to get himself out of this pickle. Was Han paying for the room? He *had* told him not to worry, but Daniel could not ask him. After all, he was a businessman who wanted to buy products from this guy; he could not let on any more than he already had that cash flow was a serious problem at the moment.

Resigned, he said, "It is a very nice room, but not what I normally go for, and certainly not what I really wanted."

"Look, you have a view from both sides of the hotel," said Han, ignoring him. He tipped the porter, who duly left.

Daniel wandered from the dining area to the main bedroom to find the largest bed he had ever seen. It was magnificent, with views right down the Bosphorus and its large picturesque suspension bridges.

"The room is big!" announced Han with a smile. "But do not worry, you will not stay here alone."

Daniel thought for a moment, his mind racing with uncertainty as he suddenly had visions of women of the night being purchased for him; something he would not tolerate.

"What do you mean, exactly?"

"I will stay here with you."

Daniel's heart sank into the pit of his stomach for the umpteenth time that day. He looked around for any sign of a second bed, or even a sofa bed, but the sitting area was decked out in rattan and there was no sign of one.

"I will collect you at 7pm," Han stated as he walked towards the door. "We will go for a meal and hit the town for an evening you will not forget."

"Oh, bloody hell!" Daniel said out loud as the door slammed closed. He had already had a day he was not going to forget in a hurry, and now he truly dreaded what Han might have in mind for that evening. As for staying in the room with him, well that was simply out of the question!

He spent the next half-hour pacing between the dining room and bedroom, looking at the views, but taking none of them in. He tried to tell himself that he must have misheard Han's comment and that he was making a mountain from a molehill, but his gut was telling him a different story.

As well as being tense, he was tired after travelling, and decided he would feel better after a shower. He got undressed and wandered into the marble bathroom, which was the size of most people's bedrooms and had a heated floor as well as a phone next to the toilet.

"Very plush," he muttered sourly. "How the hell am I going to pay for this?

The stupid fixes you manage to get yourself into! You should have listened to your doubts back in London. You're an idiot, Daniel."

He got into the shower and stood thinking as the piping hot water cascaded down his body. The words of Lucy, one of his close friends back in the UK, came back to haunt him. When he had told her how Han had crowded him in the gents, she had said laughingly, "Oh, he probably fancies you! You have to remember with some men it's women for procreation and men for fun." This had been amusing enough at the time, but now he couldn't quite push it out of his mind.

He finished in the shower, dried himself, and went to lie on the bed to think things out logically. As he lay there with his hands cupped behind his head, his imagination started to run riot, and he became more and more frightened about the predicament he was in, despite the lack of a tangible reason for it.

It was mid evening in Singapore, so he decided to phone Linda to discuss a few things with her. No doubt she would add some logic to the subject. He remembered his broken mobile, and cursed himself once more. He would have to use the hotel phone and get Linda to call him back.

CHAPTER 24

Medway Park, Singapore

Linda and Sam were still waking at all hours of the night, but they were at last beginning to get back into their routine. The neighbours had mentioned a suspicion that Salim had been over several times while they had been away, but there had been no discernible trouble, and Salvia had denied his presence.

Linda had woken at about five o'clock that morning to Sam's crying, and had gone downstairs to make a milky drink. As she heated the milk, Linda noticed that Salvia's lights were still on, and thought she would probably be as good as useless that day through being over-tired.

Sam finally went back to sleep again at about six, and Linda took him upstairs and laid him in his bed before going back to her own. She had not arranged to play tennis with her friends at the British Club until 11 that morning.

Linda woke again before Sam, and left him asleep while she had a shower and got dressed. When she went downstairs, she was surprised to see that all the shutters and windows were still closed and Salvia had not prepared breakfast. She felt a flash of annoyance, and concluded that Salvia had overslept after staying up late. She then heard shouting from the direction of Salvia's quarters and opened up the back door, calling her name. She turned to get her flip-flops to wander out there when a shrill scream cut through the air.

With that, Salvia came running out in a towel and flew towards the kitchen door, shouting, "Mem, Mem, help me, help me!"

Salim hotly pursued her as she entered the kitchen at a run. He had slipped on the damp concrete, but was now only a few metres behind her. To Linda's horror, he was brandishing a kitchen knife. Salvia shot past Linda, before grabbing her to use as a shield against Salim.

Salim's face was filled with rage as he entered the kitchen. He shouted at Linda as he brandished the knife.

"Get out of the way, or I kill you as well!"

Linda was petrified, but she responded as calmly as she could. "Salim, put the knife down! That is not going to do anyone any good!"

"It will do me good when it kill her!" he yelled, trying to take a swipe at Salvia around the side of Linda.

Linda raised her voice like she had never done before, surprising even herself. "Put that knife down now, Salim, and get out of this house!"

Salvia let go of Linda, pushing her in Salim's direction, and darted into the dining room and through the hall, where she ran into the downstairs toilet and bolted the door. Salim pushed Linda out of the way and sprinted after Salvia, dizzy with rage. Linda quickly decided that Sam was safe with Salvia in the toilet and Salim outside it, so she dashed out of the back door to her neighbours Tara and John, who were having breakfast on the terrace.

"Please help!" she screamed as she approached, bursting into tears as she got closer.

John jumped to his feet and ran towards Linda's house.

"Call the police!" he shouted back to Tara.

Linda followed, desperate to get to Sam. John ran through the kitchen and into the hall, where without a second thought he took a running tackle at Salim, who was shouting at Salvia and banging on the door, threatening to kick it in.

Salim was not expecting the attack from behind. John swept into him, planting him halfway up the stairs, and the knife tumbled onto the tiled floor with a clatter. Salim screamed like a wounded animal as John pinned him down.

"See what it's like to play with someone your own size, you pathetic bully?" John said as he locked an arm around Salim's neck and brought him to his knees.

Linda, who had been following closely behind, picked up the knife from the floor and took it to the kitchen, out of the way. John marched Salim out of the house and held him on the lawn. Salim lay still, knowing he was beaten.

Linda asked Salvia to unlock the toilet door, assuring her that Salim was under control. The maid came out reluctantly, sobbing and apologising, and Linda went to pour them all a brandy.

The police arrived within minutes and showed no mercy as they hauled Salim off to the police station, along with the knife for fingerprinting. A second police car arrived, and the long, arduous task of giving evidence started.

Tara called Linda's tennis friends and explained that she would not be able to play that morning. Linda herself soon managed to recover her senses, but it was at least two and a half hours before the police had all the details they needed. When they had gone, Linda asked John and Tara to come and join her for dinner that evening. They had originally asked her to dine with them, but she was reluctant to leave Sam. She gave Salvia the rest of the day off, and said they would discuss the situation the next morning.

***

At about 10pm, the phone rang, and Linda shot up from the table to answer it.

"Hi, honey, it's me."

At the sound of Daniel's voice, Linda burst into uncontrolled sobs.

"Honey, what's happening? What's the matter? Is Sam OK? Are you OK?"

Seeing what was going on, John approached Linda, who muttered through the sobs, "Here's John," and handed over the phone, unable to speak coherently. Tara came in and gave Linda a big hug as John spoke.

"Daniel, mate, there was a bit of a run in with Salim this morning which has frightened and shocked everyone. Nobody is hurt, and the police have taken him away."

"How's Sam?"

"Sleeping like a baby, he doesn't even know there's been any bother."

John went on to give Daniel a brief run down of the morning's events, assuring him that everything was now back to normal and they would look after Linda for him.

"Listen John, can you note down this number and get Linda to give me a ring when she is feeling a bit better?" asked Daniel earnestly.

"Sure mate, fire away."

John jotted the number down and promised he would get Linda to ring back.

CHAPTER 25

Istanbul

Daniel put the phone down and lay back down on the bed, relieved that everything was OK, but sorry he was not back at home to comfort his wife. It must have been quite the disturbance to upset Linda like that; he didn't remember ever having heard her so upset, and her distress caused his own to escalate. With nobody to sensibly discuss his worries with, the scenarios in his mind started to worsen.

What was the rented car all about? Why did Han claim it was his? Was Maya really his wife? If so, who was the other lady in London? What was Han's true relationship with Edward Lim? Was he gay, and intending to spike a drink of Daniel's and blackmail him with photos he would know nothing about?

This seemed the most likely explanation to Daniel's racing imagination, although if that was the case, where did Lim fit into it all? He was a reputable member of the Tanglin club, wasn't he? The questions kept on coming, but none could be fully put to bed. Was he being used as a pawn in some illegal game? Were they going to try and catch him in a compromising position to blackmail him?

He decided that it was probably all in his mind, and that tomorrow the boat factory would prove to be just what they needed, and all would be well. He had, however, made a decision not to go out that evening and to try and ensure that he had an early night while he had the room to himself.

He went over to his jacket and pulled his wallet from the inside pocket, from which he extracted Han's business card. He wandered back to the bed, glanced at his watch, and decided that if he was going to try and get out of dinner that evening, he had to do it now.

He picked up the receiver, pressed 9 for an outside line and dialled Han's mobile number. It was answered almost immediately.

"Hello?"

"Han, hi. It's Daniel."

"Daniel! How are you, are you enjoying your suite?"

"Well, no. The room is lovely, but I'm afraid that I'm not feeling so well."

"What is the matter?" The response came in a flat, unsympathetic tone.

"I must have eaten something on the plane; my stomach is very upset and I really do not feel well at all. I hope you don't mind if I don't take up your kind invitation to a meal this evening?"

"Yes, I do mind," came the answer "I have booked a table. I will collect you at seven o'clock."

With that, the phone was hung up. Daniel looked aghast at the handset for a second before slowly replacing it in the cradle.

"I guess that means not going out is not an option," he mumbled. He was damned if he was staying up all night, he would just eat a little of his meal, and head back to the room.

Daniel went back into the bathroom, worried. What if Han came up to the room to collect him? He'd make sure he was downstairs in the foyer in good time.

He spotted some Imodium tablets Linda had given him, and decided that if Han did come up, they would add credibility to his story. He popped two of the tablets out of their foil sheet and threw them down the toilet, ensuring that the packaging was in full view should anyone venture in there. Afterwards, he wandered back into the bedroom and flicked on the TV, hoping there would be something on to take his mind off things. The only thing that was in English was CNN, so he left that on and slowly got dressed into a shirt, chinos, tie, and a navy blazer.

At about 6pm, he decided to wander down to the hotel bar for a drink. He needed some Dutch courage and a change of surroundings before he drove himself mad with worry. Linda had not called back, so he asked reception to let her know that he was out to dinner and would be back within about three hours if she called.

Leaving the desk, Daniel wandered into the bar, which was empty except for what sounded like a couple of French businessmen at one table and a man perched on a stool studying a screen in the corner. Daniel nodded an acknowledgement to the man as he approached the bar and ordered a large gin and tonic. He turned to face Daniel and introduced himself as Ged, a Canadian who was in the soft drinks business and apparently spent his time welded to an aircraft seat somewhere between the Americas and Europe. They spent the next hour shooting the breeze. Daniel was keen to hear about Ged's experience of the business world in Turkey, and indeed the way they structured their dealings, unsure of whether his experience with Han had been unconventional.

After a while, Daniel glanced at his watch, and seeing that it was nearing 7pm, kept an eye open for Han entering the hotel. At about 7.05, he saw a familiar figure enter the foyer, so hastily said goodbye to Ged and made his way out to greet Han. His host was full of smiles, and greeted Daniel like a lifelong friend. Daniel was less happy to see him.

"How are you feeling, my friend?" Han inquired.

"Pretty lousy actually Han, and I really should be in bed, but I'll make the best of it."

"Good, good. Tonight we go to the best fish restaurant in Istanbul. It overlooks the Bosphorus."

"Sounds good," Daniel said reluctantly.

Han led the way out, Daniel following a few steps behind him. As they left the hotel, he saw the Mercedes was parked under the canopy directly outside the doors, and the doormen almost bowed as Han walked out. Daniel had noticed this same subservience at the restaurant they had eaten at earlier, and had put it down to polite serving staff, but now he was not so sure. Who *was* this guy?

As Daniel looked towards the car, he noticed someone else in it, and to his delight and relief, realised it was Maya.

"I understand you are feeling unwell?" she said sympathetically.

"Yes, unfortunately. I must have eaten something that disagreed with me, but I'm sure I'll live."

Maya laughed. It was reassuring to have her there, and he certainly felt more confident with her present. She pointed out various places of interest along the route to the restaurant, but the journey only took about ten minutes. Daniel noticed that Han's driving was considerably more subdued when she was in the car.

"Will you be coming with us to the boat factory tomorrow?" Daniel asked hopefully, realising that it would be a much more pleasant car journey that way.

"No, unfortunately I have to work tomorrow."

"Oh, that's a shame."

The restaurant was built into the side of a cliff face, and looked spectacular. Once they were out, the doorman took the keys from Han and disappeared with the Merc. Once again, he was greeted with an unusual amount of subservience, and the restaurant manager was on hand to seat them all.

"Good evening Mr Cassidy, it is our pleasure to welcome you to our humble restaurant," he said.

"Well, thank you very much. It is my pleasure to be here."

"We have the best table in the house awaiting you. Please follow me."

"This treatment is one of the things that sets this restaurant apart from others," Han explained.

The table was set into one of the bay windows, which by the look of it would open onto a small balcony during the summer. It was well laid, with silver candelabras and fresh flower decorations.

Han ordered on behalf of them all, and when the magnificent-looking crab starter arrived, it started to make Daniel's mouth water. He kicked himself for saying he was unwell, and announced that he would try at least some of the food, as it would be a shame not to. In reality, he was extremely hungry, but he did not want to claim that he had recovered from his ailments—there were still two more nights to contend with, and something told him that the sacrifice of the meal would be worth it.

Despite his claim, he demolished at least half the starter and made a good dent in the main course. The ice cream would do him good, he told them. He was able to devour all of that.

The conversation at the table consisted entirely of the culture and histories of their respective countries and families, and was nothing to do with boats or business at all. Daniel began to warm to Han slightly, and he thoroughly enjoyed Maya's company. She was intelligent, witty, and, he sensed, warm-hearted.

As they were having coffee, talk turned to what they would do for the rest of the evening. Han suggested a nightclub, but Daniel was firm, "I'm afraid you will have to leave me out, because I have to get to bed."

"No, you must come to the nightclub. It is a good place, and you will forget that you are unwell."

"No, I'm sorry. It's very kind of you, but I must insist on going back to my room."

"Han," Maya interjected, "If Daniel wishes to go to his room, why ignore his request?"

"OK, we'll take you back, " said Han, resignation colouring his tone.

"Thank you. It's gone 11.30 anyway, and I'm sure we have a long day ahead of us tomorrow."

"Yes, the drive is about three or four hours. I will collect you at 9.30 in the morning."

Han summoned the waiter and asked to settle the bill. Daniel thanked them both profusely for their hospitality and a wonderful meal.

"Will you be around tomorrow evening?" Daniel tentatively asked Maya.

"No, not tomorrow, but on Saturday we have a family dinner for Han's mother's birthday at a local hotel. We would love you to join us for that."

"That sounds splendid. Hopefully by then this wretched bug will be out of my system."

The doorman brought them their coats, and they left the restaurant and drove back to the hotel. Daniel waved goodbye, extremely relieved, then went straight into the bar for a double whisky, topping up his appetite with as many snacks as he could get hold of.

Daniel paid for his little midnight feast with his Barclaycard, then sat at the bar and ran over every little detail of what had been said that evening, analysing every comment and trying to make sense of the whole situation. It did not seem Maya had anything to hide, but he still thought that was far from the case with Han. Tomorrow would tell.

At about 12.30am, Daniel headed back up to his room, stopping at reception on the way through. Linda had indeed rung just after he had gone out. He undressed, brushed his teeth, and sat on the bed, deciding he would give her a ring in the morning. It was the early hours of the morning in Singapore, and she would surely be asleep. As much as he longed to hear her voice, she would not thank him for a call.

Despite being exhausted, Daniel had a fitful night; spending hours thinking over the various scenarios he could be faced with over the next few days. Everything seemed ten times worse in the dead of night.

CHAPTER 26

Daniel finally woke from his less than adequate night's sleep at 7.30 and hit the button for the electric curtains. They slid open silently, allowing a panoramic view of the Istanbul skyline from his bed. He flicked on CNN and got up to make a cup of tea in the kitchenette area, then took the tea and a couple of biscuits back to bed and sat looking at his surroundings, wishing that he could enjoy them.

He took a sip of his tea, and as he always did in hotels abroad, grimaced at the fact that he had to have it with UHT long life milk. When he picked up the phone to ring home, he got no reply. Linda was obviously out at one of her many social events, and was clearly OK. He showered, dressed, and made his way down to the dining area for breakfast, determined to have a good meal before the forthcoming day's events. The choice of food on offer was extensive, and Daniel did not even think twice about getting a second helping of egg, bacon, mushrooms, grilled tomatoes, sausages, and fried potatoes.

With an air of confidence, he strode out into the lobby to wait for Han. Somehow everything seemed a little better this morning, and he told himself that things would be just fine. His main fear was for his safety during the car journey with Han at the wheel.

After about five minutes, Daniel saw the Mercedes pull up outside the doors. He walked out to meet Han, who once again met him with a beaming smile and a handshake. The door closed behind him with a solid clunk—if they were going to have a prang, Daniel would rather be in nothing else, although Han's driving would probably test it.

They took off from the hotel under full throttle as expected, but it occurred to Daniel that if he engaged Han in conversation the pace might relax a little. He began to demonstrate an interest in every landmark and everything unusual he saw, but while the speeds remained the same, Han now spent more time looking sideways at Daniel as he explained something, keeping only one hand on the wheel. It was going to be a long three hours.

The weather was clear and crisp as they set off over one of the bridges over the Bosphorus. Han explained that they were going to the Asian side of Turkey, and would have to take a ferry for a short while. He did not tell Daniel of their final destination, despite being asked on more than one occasion.

Why the big secret? Daniel asked himself.

The number of half-built blocks of flats in the hills amazed him. While the top halves were open to the elements with no roofs or windows, the bottom levels were apparently inhabited. Daniel asked about this, and discovered that it was a subject Han was particularly passionate about. He felt the lack of proper planning consent had ruined the natural beauty of the countryside.

They passed through a number of tolls on the route. As they queued to go through, children of no more than nine or ten years of age would knock on the window of the car and offer a selection of old audio cassettes for sale. This happened at every toll, and Han instructed Daniel to ignore them.

As they sped down the fast lane of a congested motorway, Han suddenly swung the car straight across the inner two lanes to come off at the exit, all without dropping below 90mph. The cars in the other lanes had to take serious evasive action to avoid a collision, and showed their indignation with their horns. This made Han smile.

Sensing Daniel's unease, he said, "Do not worry, they expect this driving in Turkey. Everyone is the same."

Daniel did not comment. He had not seen anyone else make a manoeuvre like that, and it seemed to him a collision had been avoided by luck rather than judgement.

As they descended a steep slope, the view that opened up in front of them was stunning. The sun reflected off of the calm sea, and the white-capped mountain ranges on the far shore made for a superb backdrop. From Daniel's sketchy knowledge of Turkey, he assumed they must have been crossing Izmit Bay, an extension of the Marmara Sea.

"It's beautiful," remarked Daniel. Despite his cool exterior, his anxiety was beginning to return as he realised that not even he knew exactly where he was, or where he was going. "Which stretch of water is this, is it the Marmara?"

"Here is the ferry we take to the other side," said Han, failing to answer the question. "It is beautiful over there, you agree?"

"It certainly looks very impressive from here. Are we going over those mountains?"

"No, only along the bottom."

As they descended the slope, Daniel glanced down toward the ferry and noticed how ancient it was.

"Do you have a map so I can see where we are going?" he asked. "It's a shame to go on this trip and not know where I am."

"No, I have no map. You can see when you return to your hotel."

Well I guess that answers that, thought Daniel, already wondering how to memorise where he was going. He had seen no place names he recognised, and most were unpronounceable anyway.

They were one of the first cars on the ferry, and consequently were parked up near the front.

"Would you like some fresh air? It will take about half an hour to cross," said Han.

"Fine by me," replied Daniel. They got out of the car, and Han lit a cigarette as they approached the side rail.

"You will not be disappointed with our factory," he said. "I think you will be happy to do business with us."

"I certainly hope so, or else we have all wasted a lot of time and effort."

This was the first time since arriving that Han had mentioned the business in hand and it somehow reassured Daniel a little, although he was still far from happy. He decided to continue to play the upset stomach card, which gave him an excuse to be a little uncommunicative.

The temperature on the deck could only be described as bracing, and it was not long before Daniel decided to go back and sit in the car. Han finished a second cigarette and had a couple of animated conversations on his mobile phone before joining him.

As he got back in, Daniel asked, "Have you heard from Edward recently?"

"Yes, I spoke to him just yesterday, he will join us tomorrow for a ride on my boat."

"Oh, is he here in Istanbul already?"

"No, he arrives tonight."

"Which model of your boats do you have?" asked Daniel, genuinely interested.

"You will see tomorrow."

"I look forward to it. Is it one with a cabin, or a sports boat?"

"You will see tomorrow," he repeated.

They sat in silence as the ferry approached the shore, and within minutes they were on their way, although for some reason Han's driving had slowed down considerably.

The phone rang again. Han spoke in Turkish, but from his tone, Daniel could tell that he was not happy. The phone was shut off and slung into the door pocket. Nothing further was said for a while, but Daniel noticed the roads were now considerably narrower than before, with a single carriageway in each direction. He looked at the signposts, trying to make sense of where they were going. The only name that consistently appeared was that of Bursa, which was, he guessed, a city of reasonable size.

They turned off the main road onto a smaller one and continued for another 20 minutes or so. Daniel glanced at his watch and noted that they had been travelling for over three hours.

"It can't be far now?" commented Daniel.

"Still half an hour," replied Han.

They turned off the main road onto a smaller one, and accelerated on. There were no signs that Daniel could make any sense of at all. After a further fifteen minutes, they took another turn onto a dirt road and drove through a small village. Mangy dogs and dirty undernourished children ambled in the middle of the road, and Daniel was now seriously concerned as to where he was going to end up.

"This is very remote for a boat factory," he commented.

"You realise that I am kidnapping you?" came the matter-of-fact answer. There was no trace of humour in Han's voice.

Daniel's mind raced. His heart sank, and he was overcome with a wave of nausea, but he responded in the best humour he could muster, as if it was all a joke, "Well, I can tell you now you won't get very much for me!"

Han laughed, but did not comment further. Was this his idea of a sick joke? Daniel's earlier misgivings and current surroundings made the comment all too plausible, and his feelings of unease grew as he realised he had no way of contacting anyone, and absolutely no idea where he was.

As minutes of silence ticked by and the road became more and more bumpy, Daniel started to sweat, though he was trying not to show it. He began trying to memorize which turnings they had taken since getting off the ferry.

Out of the blue, on the side of the bumpy track appeared a brand new boat showroom with bold writing on the fascia that read 'United European Marine Ltd'. Daniel did not know whether to laugh or cry at the relief of seeing the building, or the stupidity of his thoughts. Either way, he was mightily relieved as they pulled up at the gates and a guard opened them to let Han pull in. Daniel got out of the car with his briefcase and took stock of his strange surroundings.

CHAPTER 27

Asian Turkey

As they got out of the car, Daniel noticed a crowd of about fifteen shabbily dressed men standing in silence towards the back of the building, watching them. Daniel looked around him. The showroom they had just driven past was very much a new façade, as the buildings behind it were older and of different sizes, all built around a central courtyard. Some of them could be classed as garages at a push, but some were more barns than anything else.

Han walked round the car and ushered Daniel into the building through a side door that entered straight into the showroom, where four sports boats sat on their trailers.

A gentleman of about fifty who spoke Turkish was introduced as Han's partner and the Managing Director. Daniel could not believe that Han had yet more partners in this business, but said nothing. The MD, whose name Daniel couldn't have begun to pronounce himself, was cleanly dressed, but did not look prosperous, his face showing the heavy tan and wrinkles of hard graft in the sun. Daniel noticed the years of grime in the creases in his hands and the down-at-heel shoes that had clearly been polished for the occasion. His shirt had worn through on the collar but was heavily starched and ironed, and his tie was faded and outdated.

There were several staff in the showroom, but they weren't salesmen. As Daniel got his bearings and took stock of the situation, he realised that they were in fact builders and decorators. A few still painted the final parts of the walls, while another nailed down the carpet in one corner.

"Is this all new?" he inquired.

"No, just a small refurbishment."

Looking at the power points and places where new wiring was showing, along with the ceiling, the lighting, and the newly undercoated woodwork, Daniel somehow doubted that it was very old at all, but who was he to judge?

Maybe Han slowed down because they weren't ready for their visitor, Daniel thought sarcastically, realising that the tense phone call was possibly due to Han demanding they get it finished, or at least respectable, in time for their arrival.

He should have known that it was not the state of décor that interested Daniel, but the boats. Turning his attention to the showroom, Daniel made a beeline for the nearest boat on show. Although it bore no resemblance to any he recognised from the brochure, it would give him an idea of the general quality.

He looked around, studying the finish, seating, woodwork, and general fittings, then he got down on his hands and knees to examine the fibreglass finish on the hull.

He was not impressed, and made no comments for at least five minutes. Han and the MD stood watching with interest and commenting quietly to themselves, but not interfering.

Daniel stood at the back of the boat, looked at them, and said, "May I?"

In response to Han's nod he climbed aboard for a closer inspection from the inside. He opened the stern lockers on either side of the transom, noting the thickness of the transom and the general lay up. It looked flimsy and agricultural, and certainly did not consist of any of the modern high-tech woven mattings used in the latest craft, but he kept reminding himself that they were being built on a budget.

Daniel finished inside without saying anything to the other two, and climbed out. As he did so, Han translated something the MD had said.

"He says this is not a new boat but an earlier model, and when you look at the other ones you will be impressed."

"I didn't say whether I was impressed or not."

"No, but what you do not say tells him a lot."

Daniel smiled and walked over to the next boat, which looked a lot more modern. He followed the same routine around this boat before moving to a smaller one sitting in the middle of the showroom.

"Could you give me a hand to turn it over please?" Both men quickly obliged and came over to help flip the boat onto its back. To Daniel's surprise, it took the strength of all three of them.

Daniel then invited Han to come over to where he was standing and look at the hull, pointing out the ripples in the finish of the fibreglass. "This would not be acceptable in the UK," he said. The MD did not come any closer; he appeared to know what Daniel was going to point out. He lit a cigarette and muttered something in Turkish, and Han gave a knowing nod and appeared to respond by explaining what Daniel was pointing out to him. The MD nodded with a slight smile and turned to look out of the window.

Daniel explained to Han that it would appear from the ripples in the hull that the moulds used were not of particularly good quality. In fact, he thought that the boats looked as if they had been made from a cheap mould cast from another boat, rather than an original mould plug.

Han agreed that the moulds were not to a very high standard, but said new ones were under construction at his other factory.

"If they were all like this, then sadly we would not be interested. However, if the boats are to be produced from new moulds, then let's look at the general construction beyond the finish of the hull, and then the new moulds."

Daniel wandered over to one of the other boats in the showroom, the largest and best looking boat of the bunch. He looked at the hull for any sign of specification plates designating the performance ratings, but could see nothing at all.

"Where do you locate the hull plate on your boats?" asked Daniel.

"This boat is new, it has not been fitted yet. Normally it would go just there," Han said, pointing to the transom.

Somehow, the longer he looked, the more the boat smacked of familiarity. Nevertheless, while the inside finish was very acceptable, the finish on the hull did not come anywhere near his expectations.

The MD wandered over, and Daniel asked Han to ask him what the lay up of the hull was, and what criteria and regulations it had been built and certified to.

"I assume all these boats meet the current CE regulations and that the factory has all of the relevant paperwork to support this?" he added. "As members of the European Union, it is illegal for UK businesses to sell any type of boat that does not meet the CE regulations in full."

Han repeated all this in Turkish for the benefit of the MD, who said something to Han and gestured towards the door that led from the back of the showroom.

"He says, 'please come and see the manufacturing and then we go to my office for a talk afterwards'."

The MD led the way towards the back of the showroom and held the door open for Han and Daniel to exit into the courtyard, then led them towards the far end.

As they stepped into the courtyard, Daniel realised how very quiet it was. All the workmen who had been watching them get out of the car had now disappeared. He could hear chatting and the faint sound of rubbing down coming from one of the sheds on the left hand side, so he presumed they had gone back to work, but there was a general lack of buzz about the place. Even in smaller volume factories, let alone ones that were supposed to produce 4000 boats a year, he was used to people running around with paperwork and deliveries, but here there was nothing. Maybe the other factory Han had spoken about was where the bulk of production was carried out, as this place simply did not have the infrastructure to do it. If that was the case, Daniel wondered why they were showing him this ghost town.

As they walked across the courtyard, Daniel asked, "How far away is the other factory you have, Han?"

"Oh, it is many miles away."

"Is most of your production done here or at the other factory?"

"Both places really."

"Are we going to see the other factory?"

"No, we won't have time to do that."

They entered one of the larger barns towards the end of the courtyard, where a number of different models of boats were lined up down the right hand side, with the left-hand side filled with a number of moulds. Daniel inspected the mould closest to him. While he was no expert, even he could see that it had not been used in a long time. Perhaps they had halted production and were trying to start again?

"This is the mould for the Phantom," Han announced proudly, pointing to a boat sitting on a trailer down the right-hand side of the barn. They all wandered towards it, Daniel examining the mould labelled for it closely on the way.

"This mould looks fairly old. Are you producing a new mould for the Phantom as well?" asked Daniel.

"Yes, yes, we have new moulds for all our models, but they are all being made at the other factory."

As they approached the Phantom, Daniel opened his briefcase and pulled a camera out..

"Wait, no, please wait a minute," Han called, disappearing with the MD behind a neighbouring boat.

"You don't mind if I take couple of pictures, do you, so that I have something I can show Luke? This model was of particular interest to us." Daniel explained with slight puzzlement.

He took several photographs of the boats, then put his camera away and clambered onto the Phantom to have a closer look at the internal finish. This time, he was not disappointed. Pleased, he looked for some form of registration plate once again, but could find none. Even if the boats were made to a higher standard from new moulds, he would have to tell his hosts that he would not entertain purchasing anything without the correct plating.

"Have you any boats that are actually in the production stage that I could have a look at?" Daniel asked.

Han muttered something in Turkish to the MD before responding.

"Apparently we show you those on the other side. We'll go there now."

They left the large shed and walked across the courtyard to where the workmen were busying themselves. The low-roofed barn also had a row of boats down one side, these all in various stages of finish. Daniel started at one end, the other two following, and worked his way down the line, examining the various stages of manufacture. He stopped occasionally to take photographs, and could not help but notice that whenever the camera was out, Han and the MD both made themselves scarce.

"Why don't I take a picture of you by one of the boats? Perhaps we could use it to promote you as our manufacturer if all goes well." Daniel suggested, already suspecting the answer.

"No, I'm very shy of camera, I do not like it. Please excuse me," said Han.

Daniel did not press him further, and instead asked what the workers were working on. They were all squatting in the middle of the floor rubbing down nondescript pieces of glass fibre, and Daniel was told they were finishing a set of louvre panels for a large order.

They finished in the shed, and Han suggested they go up to the office for a coffee and a chat. Daniel had a last look round as he walked out, not quite sure what to make of it, but relieved to know that the factory at least existed. He could now begin to relax a little.

They entered the showroom and Daniel followed them upstairs to the offices above it. They looked as new as the showroom itself; each had brand new carpet fitted and fresh paint on the walls. Brand new desks were scattered strategically around the space, but no work was being done. Daniel's own office in Singapore, as well-run and tidy as it was, had full in-trays and papers scattered everywhere, as was the way with most businesses. Either they were exceptionally good at keeping the paperwork for 4000 boats filed away, or there was very little going on. Based on what he had seen, Daniel suspected the latter.

The MD went over to a large desk in the corner of the room and pulled up a couple of extra seats before taking up his place in the large black leather swivel chair behind it. The lone secretary was dispatched to go and make coffee for the three of them.

With Han as interpreter, they sat and discussed the CE documentation necessary for the importation of the boats to the UK. As the conversation became more serious, it was apparent to Daniel that they had little idea of exactly what manufacturing standards they were supposed to meet. Luckily, he had copies of the relevant CE regulations with him, and briefly ran through a few of the fundamental basics, suggesting they photocopy them and ensure that everything conformed before spending any more money on new moulds, in case they needed changing.

The MD tried to assure Daniel that the boats met all the Turkish standards. Daniel thought these were the same as the European ones, but said he would go through them word for word to make sure. The MD listened carefully to everything that Daniel said, and made copious notes.

"Do not worry, we will not disappoint you," came the interpretation.

"He asks if you would like to go for lunch? You must be very hungry." added Han.

"That is very kind, but please explain that I'm not hungry at all due to my current illness. Under normal circumstances, I would love to accept his offer."

Han immediately started laughing, and relayed the comment to the MD, although by the length of the narrative Daniel felt Han had probably elaborated the point. The MD also started laughing.

Han then turned back to Daniel, answering his quizzical look with a stifled laugh. "I tell him that you're not hungry because you are not so well, and that you are saving yourself for me!"

A shiver swept down Daniel's spine. He could not see one ounce of humour in what Han had just said, so he just played dumb.

"I'm sorry, I don't understand," he said, shrugging the comment aside. He leaned forward and picked up one of the brochures to get back to the point. There was more laughter from the other two men, and a lengthy exchange in Turkish that made Daniel feel extremely uncomfortable.

Daniel found himself in turmoil once again, in the middle of nowhere with somebody who not only thought it amusing to pretend he'd kidnapped him, but to make jokes at a potential buyer's expense. He wouldn't be happy until he reached the hotel again.

After a further half-hour of discussions, he reluctantly accepted another cup of coffee. It was like ditch water, with very little in of the way of thirst-quenching properties, but it certainly kept him awake. Once they had finished, he thanked the MD for his hospitality, and they made their way back downstairs to the showroom, where Daniel had one final look round and took some more photographs of the boats. He shook hands with the MD and made his way to the door.

As he stepped outside and wandered in the direction of the car, Daniel glanced into the courtyard to see no sign of life at all. He could only draw the conclusion that the factory, originally run by the MD, had been in financial difficulties, and Han and Lim were investing money to develop it into a successful business. However, if that were the case, surely they would have shown Daniel the other factory? Once again, things did not add up.

Han arrived at the car shortly after him, and within seconds they were thundering off down the road.

"So, what do you think?" he asked proudly.

"It certainly gives me food for thought. It was very quiet though, I found it quite surprising."

"Yes, today was a day many of the workers were off. If we had come on a Monday, you would have seen much more activity."

"Hmm." Daniel was absorbed in the passing landscape and his own thoughts.

"Do you want to work with us?" came the blunt question after a couple of miles.

"There may be possibilities there, but I would like to see better quality hull finishes before we move much further," Daniel replied honestly. "I also only saw three boats that were similar to the models that we're interested in purchasing, and we would not be happy to proceed until we had seen all our chosen models built from the new moulds."

"Do not worry, this can be arranged. We will send one boat of each model to London from the new moulds."

"We could not possibly expect you to ship any boats to us; it isn't fair on you."

"Do not worry about fair on us. We will do this, it is not a problem." This was said as a statement rather than something that required an answer, so Daniel did not bother.

The next 15 minutes were spent in complete silence before Han's mobile phone rang. He glanced at the screen, and answered the phone in English. Judging by the conversation, Daniel assumed that it must have been Lim checking to see how the day had gone.

"Yes, very good, they like them very much and we will ship the first boats shortly. I will telephone you later." Han did not elaborate on the caller's identity after he hung up, so Daniel did not ask.

Han's driving seemed to be much more relaxed on the return journey. Daniel kept a very close eye on the direction of their travel, and was relieved that they did indeed appear to be retracing their steps.

After another few miles, the statement Daniel had been dreading all day finally arrived. "Tonight, I take you to a nightclub. You will never have a night like it."

"Thank you very much for the offer, but please understand that I am still not feeling at all well, I would ask you just to take me back to the hotel. I know that this is very boring, and I am sorry to turn down your kind hospitality, but I am afraid that resting is the only thing I feel like doing."

Han did not answer this, or even acknowledge that Daniel had spoken. They both sat in silence until they had almost reached the port, at which point Han asked," Do you want us to take the ferry back, or a different route round the coast?"

"I really do not mind. Whichever route is the quickest would be the best by me."

"We will take the coast road, which will give a different viewpoint for you."

"Thank you, that would be nice."

Daniel still wasn't sure what he had in mind for that evening. He decided he would get a taxi back to the hotel if necessary.

They followed the coast road round, and it did indeed make for very pleasant viewing. As the journey progressed Han became increasingly talkative, and by the time they reached the far side of the sea, Han was in full flow with his life history, political views, and other small talk.

As they drove through one of the small seaside villages, Han suddenly pulled onto the dirt in front of a small parade of shops.

"Do you like chocolate?" he asked Daniel.

"I don't have a very sweet tooth, but sure, I like chocolate."

"You wait here. I get something typically Turkish for you."

Daniel watched as Han walked round the front of the car, up the steps, and into a small single-fronted shop. The car was parked directly in front of it, and in the fading daylight Daniel had a good view of exactly what was happening in the interior. Daniel watched with interest as he saw Han having a laugh with the shopkeeper and pointing at various selections on the shelves before heading out of the shop with a box. He walked up the to the passenger side of the car, opened Daniel's door, and insisted that he try one of the sweets inside. Daniel duly obliged.

"Do you like?"

"Yes, it's certainly different." The sweets were ultra-sweet squares with the texture of roof insulation, and in truth, Daniel wasn't quite sure whether he liked them or not.

"Good, I knew you would."

With that, Han disappeared back into the shop. Daniel watched as more boxes of sweets were put into plastic bags and Han headed back towards the car. He showed Daniel the bags.

"These two boxes are for you and your wife, and these two are for Luke and his family," he said as he placed the boxes on the back seat of the car.

"That is really very kind of you Han, thank you."

"It is my pleasure, you are my guest."

Daniel suddenly felt a pang of guilt for not accepting his hospitality more freely. Perhaps he had completely misread the situation, but he had learned to go with his gut instinct, and things were certainly not as straightforward as they should have been.

They pulled back into the stream of traffic heading towards the centre of Istanbul; Han busy explaining the itinerary for the rest of Daniel's visit. Tomorrow, he would pick Daniel up at about 9.30, and they would go to Han's office and meet with Lim. They would then all board Han's boat for a trip on the Bosphorus, and in the afternoon Maya would take Daniel to do some shopping and see a bit of the old city. After this, she would bring Daniel directly to Han's mother's house, from where they would go out for a celebratory meal.

Daniel was relieved to hear that Maya would play a large part in the following day's proceedings, and as they approached Istanbul's centre he was once again beginning to relax. He had suddenly become quite tired, and the hunger pangs from skipping lunch had long gone. He closed his eyes to save further conversation as they approached the outskirts of the city, and within a short time they drew up at the hotel, where Han made one final attempt to entice Daniel out for the evening. After firmly declining, Daniel got out, thanked Han for the day, and wandered into the lobby.

CHAPTER 28

The evening was young, but Daniel made straight for the bar and ordered a double whisky. On an empty stomach, the whisky soon had more than the desired effect, so Daniel thought he had better go into the dining room for dinner before consuming any more. He left the bar, wandered into the lobby, and approached the reception desk on his way to the restaurant.

"Do you have any messages for me?"

"Yes, Mr Cassidy, your wife telephoned. The message was to stress that she is fine, but to ask you to call her if you're back before midnight Singapore time."

"Thank you."

Daniel decided he would go and have a quick meal in the restaurant, then retire to his room and telephone Linda. He was quickly seated in the restaurant, and ordered a large T-Bone steak and chips. He decided that he had had enough alcohol for the evening, so sipped a Coca-Cola as he waited for his meal to arrive. It arrived within fifteen minutes, and Daniel tucked into it as if he had not eaten for a month.

Once he had finished, he made his way straight upstairs to his room. He undid his tie as he walked down the corridor, and once in his room he threw it to one side and went straight over to the phone.

"Hi honey, it's me," he said as Linda answered. It would be easy to sit and chat for the rest of the evening, but he would not worry Linda with his suspicions and problems. From the sound of it, she was going to need his support, and he did not want to add to her concerns.

"Darling, how are things going?" she said. "I'm sorry if the phone call the other night worried you; there was nothing you could have done from Istanbul. Everything's under control now anyway."

"How is Sam?"

"He is just fine, full of the joys."

"What happened?"

"I'll tell you all about it when you get back. Anyway, how is everything going out there?"

"Not too bad, bit of a disappointment I guess. I'm not sure whether we will be able to do business with them or not, but it was certainly worth the visit. Have you heard from Luke at all?"

"Yes, he telephoned earlier today. He couldn't get hold of you on your mobile, so has asked me to ring him if I hear from you."

"Unfortunately I sat on my mobile and broke it." Daniel admitted. "Do you know how he got on?"

"He said that the factory was fantastic, and unless things in Turkey were absolutely perfect you would be wasting your time."

"Tell him I'll see him in England on Sunday, as arranged. If he can arrange a flight out on Monday evening, I'll be home by Tuesday."

"I can't wait, I miss you so much. What's the hotel like?"

"Too grand; I'll tell all when home. I miss you too honey, I can't wait to get back. Give Sam a big kiss for me, I'll see you both Tuesday."

"Bye for now, darling."

Daniel replaced the receiver in its cradle. He felt uplifted having spoken to Linda; it was a great relief to know that she was OK. He also felt easier in the knowledge that there was a suitable manufacturer lined up whether the Turkish boats proved to be up to scratch or not

Daniel went for a shower, telephoned reception to arrange a wake-up call for 7.30 the following morning, and drifted immediately into a deep sleep.

CHAPTER 29

Xu had been in Istanbul since well before Daniel's arrival arranging all the necessary details for his visit, although he kept his contact with Han to a minimum so as not to arouse suspicion. The news that Daniel had wanted to pay a visit to the factory had put Xu and Han into a bit of a tailspin, once again leaving them cursing Gordon, who would simply have accepted sample stock into the UK for appraisal. How easy it would have been if everything had gone according to plan!

The small glass-fibre factory they had purchased from the liquidator suddenly needed a major transformation to give it any form of credibility. It was a tall order to make a derelict factory look as if it produced 4000 boats a year in just a couple of weeks. They had focused their attentions on the appearance of the showroom and offices rather than the quality of the products they had shown Daniel, which they now knew could be their downfall.

Han dropped Daniel at the hotel and made the half hour's journey to his office further along the coast. As he drove up, he could see the lights burning inside, and knew that Xu was waiting for a full update. He locked the car and made his way up to the first floor, where Xu was looking out of one of the full-length panoramic windows with a cup of coffee in his hand.

"Didn't sound convincing," Xu said without turning around.

"What do you mean?"

"You didn't sound convincing when I spoke to you on the telephone earlier."

"Things were a bit difficult, he was in the car with me."

"How did it go then?"

"I think they will take the boats. He was unhappy with the quality of the boats we had on show, but I think I have convinced him that the ones we send to England will be from new moulds. They were still finishing the showroom when we arrived, so I had to tell him that we were refurbishing. I am not sure whether he was convinced or not, as there was very little happening at the factory. The few people they had available were working on a small number of fibreglass pieces, with not one person working on a boat mould or hull. I could have strangled them there and then. "

"I need to know whether he is going to play ball or not, because if not, we will have to put alternative plans into play tomorrow. It will be our only chance. Are we doing business with them, or not?"

"I will ensure that we wrap up a deal. I do not know why you're worrying so much. After all, he hardly knew which country we were in when we went to the factory, let alone where it was."

"He is not stupid, that's why I'm worried! He is so suspicious of everything that he could jeopardize the entire future of our business. I have invested a large amount of money in this, and I intend to see it succeed, so we must ensure that it does. I will leave you to think about it overnight, and I will do the same. Tomorrow, we must make the decision either to continue with Daniel's company, or to eradicate the problem and find somebody less suspicious in England."

"Yes, I agree with you. I'm sure that after the first few boats arrive in England, they will sell them and make a profit, and all will be fine from then on. I think they are just cautious because they have not dealt with us before. They would probably be the same with anybody, we are just reading more into everything than we need to."

"For your sake, I hope you're right, but we'll reach the final decision in the morning. What time do we meet?"

"About 10.15."

"Is Sunjin ready with the boat?"

"Yes, he is all ready. We will be out for a couple of hours or so."

With that, Han left. He took out his frustration on the car during the journey home, revving the 2-litre engine at every opportunity. He was fed up with Lim's negativity, but understood that caution was necessary.

CHAPTER 30

The following morning brought the beginnings of a clear day in Istanbul, with temperatures hovering around freezing, a beautiful deep blue sky, and no wind as Daniel's early morning alarm call went off. He had slept as if he had been on tranquilizers, and it took him some time to muster the courage to get up.

He finally threw himself out of bed, pushed the button to open the curtains, and made himself a cup of tea. He then sat back in the in bed, pondering the coming day's events. He was looking forward to some time out on the water, and it would be interesting to see Istanbul from such a unique viewpoint. He was unsure what type of boat Han owned, but he felt sure that it would be one of the larger models they made, hopefully with a cabin for some protection from the cold. He was also looking forward to the afternoon with Maya, and seeing a little more of the city. Yes, he was a much happier person this morning, and although he had one more night to stay, he felt that his 'illness' could probably have improved a little today. After all, that evening's events were already planned, and he felt more secure for it.

He whistled to himself as he showered; something he had not done since arriving, and once again took full advantage of the superb breakfast on offer. Afterwards, he waited in the lobby for Han to arrive and contemplated the end of the stay. He had already decided that if there was a problem with the hotel bill, he would simply have to get Vera to telegraph some money into the hotel's bank account. He was quite convinced that the room rate would have been in the region of $1000 per night, and while he was extremely upset the thought of spending this money, he would just be happy to get out.

Daniel had been waiting for at least half an hour when he saw the familiar Mercedes pull up to the front door of the hotel. He did not wait for Han to get out of the car this time, but walked straight out to get into the passenger side. Han was full of smiles once again, and immediately asked after Daniel's health.

"I feel a little better today, thank you very much," he replied. "I'm sure that the fresh air out on the boat will help."

"Good! We will go to the office first and collect Edward. He has already arrived, and that is why I am a little bit late, I'm sorry."

Because they were running late, Han decided to stretch his racing skills to the limit, and within half a kilometre Daniel had to close his eyes at almost every turn of the wheel. They soon reached some densely populated single carriageways, much to Daniel's relief, and followed the coast road round the edge of a large harbour. Daniel looked out at the various shapes, sizes, and conditions of the boats moored in the middle of the harbour with worry. A little further on, the pontoons of a marina jutted out from the shore. On the left-hand side of the road, the shops were becoming progressively smarter and the showrooms grander.

"Is your boat one of these in the marina?" Daniel asked hopefully.

"No, it is not one of these."

He assumed that it must be one of the smaller sports boats bobbing about on their swinging moorings further out, and thought he recognised a couple of boats similar to those he had seen at the factory.

Daniel was busy studying some of the expensive-looking shops to the left of the road when Han parked abruptly on the right. He opened the window on Daniel's side of the car and leaned across. There were a number of extremely large motor yachts moored against the wide pavement. The yacht opposite had its passerelle down, and a man of about 50 stood on its fly bridge. The boat was extremely grand, but very sleek. Han shouted at the gentleman on the fly bridge, and the pair exchanged a few words in Turkish. After a minute or so, Han indicated left, closed the window, and they pulled back into the stream of traffic.

"Friend of yours?"

"Yes, actually he is my captain."

"Your *captain*?" Daniel said incredulously. "You mean that is your boat?"

"Yes, you like it?"

"It looks superb! What is she?"

"She is an Italian Ferretti, 82 feet long. I had her built last year at a cost of $2.5 million." He announced this almost arrogantly, without a trace of humility.

"I very much look forward to seeing her more closely."

"Yes, but first we'll go to my office and collect Edward. He is looking forward to seeing you again."

As the flow of traffic crept forward slowly, Daniel turned in his seat to have another look at the yacht, which he had to admit was totally beyond anything he had imagined. However, this brought with it further doubts; he wondered how Han could afford a yacht like that from a small boat building business. Either the other factory was as busy as Han described, in which case Daniel should have been shown it, or his host had fingers in other pies, not all of them necessarily legitimate.

A new sense of unease crept over Daniel. In what way could he be being used, and for what? Almost as soon as the thought entered his head, he told himself not to be stupid. It was probably just family money, and he should enjoy the experience. However, his mind could not let go of the thought that Han was involved with something far greater than just boat building, and that he could be in some sort of danger.

Approximately four miles on, they pulled up at the side of the road. Han switched off the ignition and announced that they were at the office. Daniel glanced at the buildings on the shore and got out of the car. He followed him across the road and into one of the many doorways, which led up some stairs and opened out into a hallway. A secretary met them at the top of the stairs, took their coats, and offered Daniel a coffee, which he accepted with thanks. Han showed Daniel into one of the offices and asked him to have a seat, then went into one of the other offices, where Lim was waiting.

"What are your thoughts?" asked Lim.

"I think he will be fine. We should just carry on as normal."

"I hope you're right, but I don't trust him; I'm sure he's cottoned on to us. If anything comes to light this morning that makes us think he will jeopardise things, we must be ready."

"But if anything happens to him, we will have the best police forces from Singapore to Scotland Yard sniffing around, and that is the last thing we need. We are better just letting things quietly drop."

"You may be right. Anyhow, let me come and greet our friend."

Daniel stood at the full-length window marvelling at the panoramic view of the harbour that trailed on down the Bosphorus. Suddenly, he heard the door open behind him and turned to see Lim walking towards him with an outstretched hand and a smile. Daniel smiled back, and walked over to shake his hand.

"Edward, it's very nice to see you again. How is Singapore?"

"Daniel," Lim acknowledged with a slight bow. "Singapore is very wet at the moment, it is good to enjoy the climate here."

"Yes, I'm sure. When did you arrive?"

"Only last night, so I am suffering a little with jet lag. I hope Han has been looking after you during your stay?"

"Yes, he's been looking after me very well, thank you."

"Good. Tell me Daniel, what did you think of our small factory?"

"I have to say, it was a little quieter than I expected, and the quality of the hulls was not as good as I would have liked to see. However, Han assures me that there are new moulds being built, and if this is the case then maybe we can arrange something once all the CE ratings are surpassed and certificated. Please don't think we are trying to be awkward; this would be the same with any importer in any European country. All I am trying to do is to make sure we all do our jobs properly. After all, the last thing any of us want is the boats being stuck at Customs due to having incomplete documentation."

"OK, I see. So when the new moulds are done, you will have no problem?"

"Yes. It is obviously something I have to discuss with my partner, as we are looking at other manufacturers at the same time, but as with all things we will have to throw price and quality into the melting pot and make sure that the package we come up with is the one we're happy with."

"I understand. Han and I are quite convinced that we will be doing many years of profitable business with you."

"That would be very nice, let's hope so."

"When you have finished your coffee, we can make our way to the boat."

Daniel finished what he had left of his coffee, and they headed out of the office. He followed Han across to where the Mercedes was parked, while Lim headed off in a different direction to collect his own car.

As Han turned the Mercedes around in the side road, a brand-new Jaguar XK headed down the road towards them.

"Ah, here's Edward now," announced Han, pointing at the Jaguar.

"Does he keep that in Istanbul just for the short periods that he spends here?" Daniel replied incredulously.

"Yes. He says he has more opportunity to drive it here than in Singapore."

"Well, I can believe that, but he has more opportunity to write it off here too!"

Han laughed, and they drove off. They followed Lim the few miles back to the boat and parked behind him, opposite the stern of the yacht. The captain was standing on the aft deck waiting to greet them.

As Daniel walked aboard, he tried to take in every detail, dumbstruck at the beauty of the vessel. It was truly magnificent in every respect. The aft deck floor was a beautifully laid teak, and the fixtures and fittings were better than any Daniel had seen on a boat before.

Han had a quick discussion with the captain, and then led Daniel and Lim into the main saloon, where Daniel was almost at a loss for words. The seating was finished in a cream Italian leather, and the latches and fasteners were all finished in gold, contrasting with the polished walnut panelling. The cream carpet in the main saloon was so thick Daniel thought that he would sprain his ankle if he fell off of it.

One of the cupboards along the side of the saloon was open, revealing a top-of-the-range Bang & Olufsen hi-fi system, which, Han was quick to point out, was plumbed throughout the boat. Han pushed the button on a remote control unit and a walnut fascia slid aside, exposing a 40-inch LCD widescreen television. Within a few minutes, Han had inserted a DVD into the player next to the television and was demonstrating the superb sound quality of the system. Daniel had to admit that it was the best he had seen—he could have played with that alone for hours on end.

They then moved on to the galley area, which was all finished in limed oak with the surfaces and backdrop in what looked like solid marble. It was naturally very well appointed;

with everything one could need, including a full height fridge freezer and microwave oven. Opposite the galley was a large dining table with seating for twelve.

The next stop was the helm area, which had seating for eight people, all forward facing. The dashboard alone was approximately two metres wide and loaded with instruments, dials, and gadgets of all shapes and sizes, along with the very latest satellite navigation aids. They then made their way down the forward staircase to the cabins, which were as fine as Daniel had come to expect. Every cabin had an en-suite with plenty of room.

They made their way through a door into the engine room, where two huge Caterpillar diesel engines sat on either side.

As Daniel looked around, he muttered, "It really is fantastic."

Han overheard and responded, "You too can have one of these if business goes well. Perhaps we sell many boats next year!"

Daniel laughed. "I like your optimism, Han!"

They left the engine room through a door at the other end to enter another section of the boat with three more cabins. These, Han informed him, were the crew's quarters. The three men left via a staircase, and found themselves back up on the aft deck.

"That was quite a tour! Thank you, Han."

"I am very pleased you like it. Now we can show you how she performs."

Han went forward to issue some instructions to the captain, who immediately fired up the engines. After a few minutes of warming up, they cast off the lines and headed down the Bosphorus, pootling out at a leisurely 12 knots until the harbour was but a speck in the distance before the captain felt it prudent to open up the two Caterpillars.

Daniel decided to wander outside, but it was only as he opened the rear sliding doors that he realised how well insulated the inside was. The noise outside was thunderous, but the deep roar of the engines was far from unpleasant. The temperature, on the other hand, was, and he soon retreated back inside.

Their captain, who appeared to be the only member of staff on board, left Han in control of the boat while he made a hot drink for everybody. Daniel gratefully accepted the offered cup of tea, more than anything to warm his hands on. Before long, he needed to use the toilet, and out of courtesy advised Han of his intentions before heading below.

"Wait, I come with you and show you."

"No, that's not necessary, I have used many sea toilets in the past."

"OK, you know where to go?"

"Yes, I remember, thank you."

Daniel made his way down the forward staircase, into the master cabin and through into the bathroom. While he stood at the bowl, he looked at all the gadgetry attached to the marble basin and shower units. He was impressed. When he had finished, he looked for the toilet flush, but could not make sense of anything. The larger motor boats he had used had had a very obvious plunger-type handle next to the bowl, which, when manually pumped, sucked raw sea water into the bowl and flushed it. He finally noticed a small button down the side of the bowl itself, and assumed it must be the flush facility. Although he thought it was in an odd place, he bent down and pushed the button. He heard a motor whirr into life, and quickly removed his finger. The motor stopped, and he pushed the button again, but this time kept it depressed. Within milliseconds, a huge gush of high-pressure water shot upwards from a small hole in the back of the bowl. It caught Daniel squarely in the face, completely drenching him.

He let go of the button in shock, jumping backwards as if he had just been shot, then grabbed a towel from the rail and quickly dried the worst of it off. Daniel looked in the mirror, confused and embarrassed. He did not dare push any more buttons, and after about five minutes of drying made his way back up the stairs with his clothes still damp. Luckily, Lim and Han were deep in conversation when he got back into the main saloon, so he quietly made his way to the back to his helm seat and sat down to take in the view.

Han came out with Lim after a few minutes and started pointing at some of the historical buildings along the waterfront. Daniel lapped up the information while Lim disappeared back to the main saloon with complete disinterest. It was apparent that they had had an argument of some sort while Daniel had been below; the atmosphere was tense.

After a while, Han turned to Daniel. "Maya will be waiting for you in about one hour, so we have to turn round now."

He gently turned the Ferretti in a wide arc, and they headed back on the other side of the waterway. The only chatter heard during the last hour of the trip was Daniel's questioning about various monuments, palaces, or other interesting buildings that they saw en route.

The captain re-emerged approximately ten minutes from mooring and took over the helm. As they neared the bank, Daniel could see Maya standing on the pavement, waiting to see them in. As the captain went astern into the mooring, Daniel jumped off to throw the lines aboard and greet Maya. They stood and talked while the others gathered their possessions and made ready to leave.

CHAPTER 31

Lim followed Han off the boat after a few minutes, and they walked up to where Daniel and Maya were talking. Lim approached Daniel and proffered a hand.

He did not look Daniel in the eye, and simply said, " I must go now. I will see you back in Singapore," before muttering something to Han and then making his way back to his car.

Han, obviously feeling guilty for Lim's lack of communication, apologised and explained that Lim had a lot on his mind at the moment. Daniel sensed that there was probably a lot more to it than Han was suggesting, but did not pry further. Instead, he went back on board to thank the captain for his hospitality before making his way back to the pavement.

"Maya will look after you for the rest of the day. Maybe you can keep an eye on her for me to ensure she does not spend too much money!" Han said in jest, raising his eyebrows at Maya as he did so. "I too have a meeting now, so I will see you this evening for the dinner with my mother."

"I look forward to it. Thank you for the trip on your magnificent boat; I learned a lot." Daniel got into the passenger side of Maya's car as Han wandered back up to the Mercedes.

***

Daniel felt much more comfortable with Maya's driving than he did with Han's. As Han sped past them, Maya made a comment that did not come as a surprise to Daniel.

"I did not like the Mercedes before, but now I have driven it a couple of times, it is really a very nice car."

"What happened to his BMW?" Daniel asked.

"Oh, it is so old it keeps on breaking down. That is why he rented the Mercedes for your visit."

Daniel was relieved to hear that the BMW, did in fact exist, and observed that Han's comments about owning the Mercedes must be nothing but bravado, though he could not help but wonder why somebody who owned a $2.5 million yacht had to rent a car because his own was old and unreliable. It simply did not make sense, but it would be unfair to push Maya for answers.

Within twenty minutes, they had arrived at the White Centre and parked in the multi-storey car park. He found himself impressed by the general quality of the goods on display, and within the hour had made several purchases, mostly items of clothing. Maya, he noted, refrained from spending money, but was able to give Daniel good advice when he was indecisive about what to buy for Linda. They left the White Centre on foot and wandered around some of the local streets, which turned out to be a less pleasurable experience. They were hampered by begging children at every corner tugging at their clothes and asking for money; it was all very different from Singapore.

Later that afternoon, when they had been walking for several hours, Maya suggested they went for a coffee at a little coffee shop she could recommend. It was situated inside a very old building that was heavily beamed inside and decidedly cosy on such a cold afternoon. They sipped at cappuccinos while Maya gave Daniel a general insight into life in Istanbul, telling him of her own upbringing. It was apparent from the gaps in her responses to Daniel's questions about her married life that she knew very little of Han's business.

As they left, Daniel noted that the afternoon had been the most relaxed since he had arrived in Turkey. He wished the whole stay had been as pleasurable. Time marched on as they pulled out of the car park, but Maya announced that it was only a fifteen-minute drive to Han's mother's apartment.

"We should arrive exactly when Han arrives," she said.

As they waited in the traffic on the way out of the city centre, Daniel decided to probe a little into Han's family background.

"Does Han's mother have an occupation, or does she lead a life of leisure now?" he asked.

"No, Eila does not have to work; her husband left her very well provided for. She spends most of her time travelling the world. In fact, she has only just returned from Australia, and she's leaving for America in three weeks' time for a cruise."

"Very nice too! Her husband was a wealthy man, then?"

"Not particularly, but he had a good job. They were able to give Han a good upbringing, and when he died, he had a good life insurance policy. There is no doubt that she will never want for anything again."

Daniel thought about the boat, and the two and a half million needed to buy it. It was now apparent that it hadn't come from family wealth, and once again, his suspicions were aroused.

As they approached the outskirts of the city, the traffic began to thin, and it became clear that they were entering a neighbourhood a far cry from the half-built apartment blocks on the other side of the city. As they descended a hill on one of the quiet suburban roads, Daniel could see the Mercedes parked near the bottom.

"He has beaten us here. We will park behind him," Maya announced as she pulled the Volvo into the kerb. As they approached the front door, it opened and Han greeted them. Eila's house was built into the side of a hill, set back from the road. It was no architectural masterpiece from the outside, but nor were any of the houses. They were shown through into the sitting room, where Han's mother greeted them.

She was tall, younger looking than Daniel had expected, and expensively but tastefully dressed. Han opened a bottle of champagne they had put on ice, and they toasted Eila's birthday, which Daniel guessed was probably about her 60th. As they started to talk, it was obvious that she was indeed very well travelled, and they were soon lost in chatter about various parts of the globe.

After about an hour, it was time for them to depart to the restaurant. As they drove, Daniel began to see a more human side of Han. Eila was very fond of her son, and the feeling was mutual. On noticing this, Daniel's confidence began to grow, and he even started to risk a bit of banter at Han's expense. To his relief, Han took it well. Daniel was definitely beginning to feel better now, and told the others that he was in a fit state to enjoy a full meal that evening.

They left the car in one of the side roads, and as time was on their side, spent half an hour wandering around the waterfront streets, which were waking up for the evening and already busy. The restaurant Han had booked for the birthday celebration was, it turned out, extremely large, taking up a good percentage of the ground floor of one of the bigger hotels. They were shown to their table right away, but no sooner had they sat down than Han's mobile rang. He spent the next fifteen minutes away from the table talking to the caller. By the time he came back, the rest of the group had already decided what to order. He sat down and had just made his choice when his phone rang again. As before, he disappeared from the table for a further fifteen minutes. When he returned the second time, Maya decided she had had enough of this, and instructed him to turn his phone off. The request did not appear to go down well, and halfway through the starter it was apparent that Han had not observed it, as he disappeared to a corner of the restaurant for a third time. When he returned, Eila chastised him, and Han apologised for the interruptions. He explained that he had a big business deal that was not going as smoothly as he would have liked, and he needed to sort it out.

The rest of the meal was relatively uneventful until the dessert arrived, at which point Han said he would be back in five minutes. Daniel did not mind this, as he found the company of the two ladies far more stimulating, particularly as Han appeared to be in a very vacant and distant mood.

When Daniel had finished his dessert, he excused himself and wandered in the direction of the main foyer in search of a bathroom. On the other side of the foyer, he noticed Han standing with two swarthy-looking men. The three of them appeared to be involved in a heated discussion, and Daniel kept well out of their way as he made his way to the gents and back to the table.

They were all enjoying coffee and mints when Han finally returned to the table, apologising for his absence. It was immediately noticeable that the apology was not acceptable to either Maya or Eila, but in order to avoid spoiling the evening, they continued to chat and enjoy themselves for a good hour after they had finished their meal. Han visibly began to relax, and Daniel had to admit to feeling slightly sorry for him. If his problems were bad enough to disturb an evening such as this, then he was obviously a fairly worried man.

He was feeling weary by the time they left the restaurant, so Maya offered to drive him back to his hotel to rest, as they would collect him at 9am. Daniel happily accepted, and once they had arrived at the hotel, said goodbye to Maya and made his way straight up to his bedroom, where he enjoyed a long hot shower before collapsing into bed. He knew London was behind the local time zone, so he thought he would see if he could get hold of Luke to find out how he had got on.

His mobile went to voicemail, and there was no reply from the house phone either, which suggested that he had gone out for a meal. Daniel rolled over, and with the knowledge that there was nothing further to worry about that night, swiftly fell into a deep sleep.

CHAPTER 32

After leaving the boat in Istanbul, Xu made his way back to the office to see Han before flying back out to Singapore via his hometown of Kuala Lumpur, entering via the side entrance. He was always careful about how he contacted Han and where he was seen with him, and used the alias of Edward Lim—the name shown on his false passport—in Istanbul as well.

"You certainly picked the wrong partners for this one." Xu told Han, laughing coldly. "You told me they would not be very thorough, but they wanted to know the ins and outs of everything, and the 'factory' made us look like fools. You'd better get the back-up in place mighty quick, because we are running out of time. The most critical part was left to you to organize, and now it's becoming a fucking cock-up. You'll get things straight from here on in, or else! Do I make myself clear?"

"Yes perfectly," Han quaked. "It will all run smoothly, believe me."

"Unfortunately, I am going to have to. You know the consequences if you fuck up further."

Xu turned from the window and walked to the door. "I leave tonight for Singapore. By the time I get there, I expect to hear some good news from you. In the meantime, I will contact Daniel and Luke to see if they are still an option."

He drove straight from the office to the airport, where he returned his rented XK and got on the courtesy bus to the terminal. Within a couple of hours, he would be airborne, heading for Kuala Lumpur.

***

Han wandered over to the drinks cabinet, poured himself a large whisky and went back to his desk to think of the best way to co-ordinate things. He still hoped that Daniel's company would agree to be the consignee, but he needed a reliable back up. He would see if Eugene, a colleague and old friend in who owned a small second hand car yard in northwest London, had any ideas. Plan one was still the preference, as it would look far more conventional and raise no questions, but he had to do something. In any case, Eugene had been tasked with dispatch and general logistics once boats started to come into the country, and Han was set to have introduced him as the buyer for the boats when they arrived.

CHAPTER 33

Daniel's sleep was soon interrupted by the sound of knocking, which he initially assumed was part of his dream. As it stopped and restarted, he was thrown into the realms of semi-consciousness and sat bolt upright in bed, listening. It was dark, and for a few moments, he was on the verge of panic as his brain raced to try and work out where he was, and what time it was. He flicked on his bedside light and glanced at his watch; 12:30 am. He had been in bed for only three quarters of an hour, and felt awful.

The knocking started again in earnest, making Daniel jump. He leapt out of bed and made his way through the dining area into the main hall of the suite. He could see light coming through the peephole in the door and approached it gingerly. Perhaps there was an emergency, and someone was trying to inform him he needed to leave his room? As he looked through the spy hole, reality set in once again. Han was standing on the other side of the door with two heavily made-up women.

Daniel quickly withdrew his head and stood absolutely still, his heart pounding. He continued to stand rooted to the spot as the knocking continued with more fervour. He wondered how on earth to get out of this predicament, and made his way back to the bedroom, where he sat on the end of the bed, his mind racing. He knew that if he let them in, he would not be able to get rid of them, and the consequences did not bear thinking about.

The knocking stopped, and Daniel started to make his way towards the door again when a shrill ring from the phone broke the silence. There was no way he was going to answer it. As it continued to ring, he checked the spy hole in the door, and was horrified to see that the two women were still there.

Daniel began to panic, wondering what would happen next. As he stood by the door, he realised that as Maya was bringing him back to the hotel, Han must have gone off to collect these women. He kicked himself for having admitted to feeling better, and again wondered what this was all in aid of. Perhaps blackmail was somehow on the agenda? In any case, he was married, and wanted none of it.

He heard chattering outside the door and took another look to see Han appear with one of the hotel bellboys in tow. Daniel could see the bellboy laugh at whatever Han was telling him, and noticed that he had a swipe card in his hand.

Daniel bristled. He was going to have to confront the situation, and it would be better done while there was a member of the hotel staff there, he supposed. The bellboy knocked on the door, and almost before he had withdrawn his hand Daniel threw the door open, rubbing his eyes as if he had just been woken. He decided attack was the best form of defence.

"What the hell's going on? it's one o'clock in the bloody morning, and I was fast asleep! What on earth do you want? What is the meaning of this?" he asked, gesturing disdainfully to the two women.

Han muttered something in Turkish to the bellboy, who laughed and started to retreat.

"Whatever it is you want, it will have to wait until the morning," said Daniel. "I'm in no mood for games, and I'm going back to bed." He slammed the door behind him. He heard Han call to the bellboy to open the door, but his footsteps continued, much to Daniel's relief. Han started knocking again, and Daniel put the security chain on the door before opening it a crack.

"Look Han, I don't know what you're playing at, but please just leave me in peace," he said. "I wish to get some sleep."

"The girls...it will be fun, I got them specially."

"I don't care how specially you got them, I am not interested. Now please go away! I will see you in the morning."

"OK, but you will regret it," Han said threateningly, with a look so cold it could have turned the Mediterranean to ice.

Daniel closed the door as a shiver ran down his spine. He was now wide-awake. After he unplugged the phone from its socket, he sat on the bed watching CNN, his mind churning over the situation. He thought seriously about doing a midnight dash to the airport and getting on the first aircraft out of Turkey, but it was late, he was tired, and while it seemed like a good option right now, he was sure he would be able to look at it more objectively in the morning. He turned the TV and lights off and rolled over to try and get some sleep, though it now seemed far away. His imagination once again ran riot, particularly at Han's last comment.

CHAPTER 34

Daniel had his usual cup of tea in bed before starting to pack for the return journey. He was looking forward to going home, but he hoped to be able to afford to get a room like this with Linda and Sam at some stage to enjoy it fully as a family. Because of the bulk of the boxes of sweets, he decided to put two boxes in his suitcase and the other two in his hand luggage.

As Daniel packed, he wondered whether Han would turn up that morning to pay the hotel bill. If he did, would Daniel be taken to the airport, or would Han have something else in store, like an 'accidental' drowning in the Bosphorus?

He left his packed belongings in the room while he went down to breakfast—where he managed to force down some cereal and a little fruit—then retrieved them and started to make his way back down to the foyer.

When he was halfway across it, Han turned around and saw Daniel walking towards him, and immediately dropped his gaze. Daniel dropped his cases and shook his extended hand, but could not bring himself to return the smile Han offered.

"How are you? I am sorry for last night, I got carried away. Maya is in the car; please do not say anything. She thinks I was at my mother's for longer."

"I will not say anything to Maya, of course, but I think you have a super wife, who quite honestly deserves better. As far as I'm concerned, though, it's a closed chapter."

"Thank you. If we can put it to history, then let's go and enjoy the morning."

"OK, but first I have to go and pay my bill."

"No need, it is already settled."

"That's good of you, thank you." Daniel managed a faint smile, more from relief than anything else.

Han had left the Mercedes outside the hotel with the engine idling, and as they approached Daniel could see Maya in the passenger seat. She greeted him with a smile.

"How was your night? You must have slept well."

"Yesterday evening was wonderful; how could one fail to sleep well after that?"

Daniel almost thought he saw Han physically relax at his comments, and smiled to himself. They took off towards Topkapi Palace, where they were due to spend the morning before going on to the airport. Maya pointed out her hospital on the way, and indeed did most of the talking in the car that morning. Han was unusually quiet, probably due to his conscience.

They parked a short distance from the Palace and enjoyed the cold, bracing fresh air as they walked up the hill towards it. Daniel was fascinated by history, and as they entered the outer walls, he found himself determined to forget about the previous night's events and enjoy the morning, making the most of the short time he had left in Istanbul.

They wandered slowly through rooms full of memorabilia, making their way to the inner chambers of the Palace from which the Sultan had ruled the Ottoman Empire in the days of Constantinople. It was truly fascinating and as if the last Sultan could have walked out only days earlier. After their tour, they made their way to one of the Palace coffee shops for refreshments. Han would not look him in the eye, but Maya chatted away happily, clearly enjoying the morning as much as Daniel was.

Much too quickly for Daniel's liking, it was soon time to head for the airport. They walked briskly back to the car, and within a short time were drawing up at the departures drop-off. Maya was insistent that they should have a drink with him before he left, but Daniel had been equally insistent that this was not necessary and that he would go through Immigration and sit and read instead. They stood outside the car, where Maya kissed Daniel goodbye and Han shook his hand.

"It has been good to see you, thank you for visiting. We look forward to supplying the boats," he said.

"Well, thank you very much for your hospitality, it has certainly been a different experience. As for the boats, let me know when you have the new moulds ready and I will see what we can do."

"Do not worry, we will sort it out for you. You will be very happy with what arrives, it is my guarantee!"

Daniel ignored the last comment, knowing perfectly well that he'd made it clear that there was a lot more work to be done on the boats before he and Luke could accept them. He picked up his bags, said goodbye to them both once again, and headed into the airport terminal. As the Mercedes disappeared from view, an overwhelming sense of relief overcame him, his mood lifting.

He glanced up at the departures board and headed to check-in at a leisurely pace. He then wandered through to the departure lounge, where he browsed through the duty-free, which included variations of the Turkish sweets Han had bought. He decided to buy a further box for his parents. They were, after all, a bit different.

Once he had finished shopping, Daniel sat down and opened his book, but as he started to read the first page, he was flooded with fatigue, so went to order a coffee and watch the world go by until the flight was called.

As the announcement came over the tannoy, he made his way to the relevant gate, where a pretty British Airways hostess was greeting people. As Daniel walked past, she smiled at him

"Good afternoon sir, welcome to British Airways. Can I ask if you are carrying anything for anybody else?"

"Good afternoon. No, I am not," Daniel said with a smile. As he stepped into the tunnel leading to the aircraft, he realised what an oddity the question was. He missed a step as an unpleasant thought occurred to him, immediately followed by a wave of nausea.

What was in the sweets? Once again, Daniel's imagination let rip, and by the time he reached his seat, he was perspiring with worry. His mind leapt back to a book he had once read called *Midnight Express*; in which somebody caught trafficking drugs had been put in a Turkish jail. If this *was* a set-up, Daniel decided he would rather get arrested in England, where there was more likelihood of people understanding the truth of what had happened.

Catching himself as he sat down, Daniel tried to pull his brain into order. The store had appeared to be a standard sweet shop, and everything had been wrapped and sealed. He chastised himself for being daft, and tried to force the issue from his mind.

The tug began to push the aircraft back, and within ten minutes they were airborne. Once they were in the air, Daniel began to relax with the aid of a whisky and ginger ale. It went against his normal policy, but he decided he deserved it; it was after all a relatively short flight. Before long, the fatigue returned, and he soon fell asleep on a pillow wedged between the seat and the window pillar.

***

The flight became increasingly bumpy as they approached Heathrow, and it was no surprise to hear that the weather was wet, windy, and only four degrees Celsius. In the crosswinds, the landing was particularly heavy, leaving Daniel marvelling at how the tyres withstood such punishment.

As they taxied towards their gate for disembarkation, the stewardess gave the routine speech detailing how far the airport was from the centre of the city and the various ways to get there, as well as where to go for onward reservations. The aircraft came to a halt, and everybody clambered to the aisles to retrieve their goods from the overhead lockers. They waited for a further five minutes for the doors to open before an announcement came over the tannoy.

"Ladies and gentlemen, Her Majesty's Customs and Excise are waiting outside the aircraft doors, please ensure that you have your passport readily available for inspection as you exit the aircraft. Thank you."

This was another new one on Daniel, and his heart began to beat so heavily he could almost see his shirt moving. If he sought confirmation of his suspicions, then this was surely it.

What the bloody hell should I do now?

The only thing he could do was to be perfectly honest; he was, after all, completely innocent.

The column of people on the far side of the aircraft started to move first, but within minutes, his aisle was shuffling forwards to the door, where a female officer in a dark Customs uniform stood checking the passports of everybody that stepped off the aircraft. She glanced at Daniel's and quickly handed it back.

"Please continue, Mr Cassidy."

Daniel continued towards the main walkway, where to his surprise, there was a further queue. Two more Customs officers stood at the top of the gangway, accompanied by a Weimaraner sniffer dog. He was once again plunged into a state of complete panic, and on the verge of fainting, but he wandered on, not knowing whether to say anything voluntarily or not. The dog had a good sniff around Daniel's hand luggage, but he was allowed to continue, which gave him a moment's relief until he realised that they would wait to pick him up until he had his main luggage from the hold. He slowly picked his way towards baggage reclaim, not really knowing what was in store for him.

CHAPTER 35

Grant Woodward had worked for HM Customs for the last 15 years, and was now head of the Drugs Squad based in central London. During his time with Customs, he had seen a multitude of imaginative ways that criminals tried to profit, and had heard all the excuses, as well as seen the damage that their greed caused to lives. He was a seasoned officer of impeccable integrity, deeply respected by all those around him, and nobody questioned his judgment or authority.

Gill Bordeman was one of the team leaders working with Woodward. She had been with Customs for eight years herself, and was equally well respected by those below and above her. She was set for greater things, and it was expected she would take over from Grant when the time came.

Both officers were monitoring a developing situation that had been brought to their attention by Turkish intelligence, who had been tipped off about a possible large drugs deal. Turkish authorities had been monitoring the situation for approximately three weeks, and had the suspected ringleader under surveillance. As in many cases, the tip-off could be from somebody trying to cause trouble because of a grudge that he or she was bearing, but all leads had to be followed up, and there seemed to be a reasonable amount of truth to this one.

When Han had collected Daniel Cassidy in Istanbul, Turkish authorities had set to work to find out who he was and where he came from. These details had been passed to Gill in London, and her team carried out the rest of the research. They now knew most of Daniel's movements from the previous few weeks, and indeed had had Singaporean authorities doing some homework over there. He did not even have so much as a parking ticket to his name, and certainly did not frequent the company of any known villains. It was a mystery to the team what his involvement with Han was, but they felt it could only have been money-motivated.

Gill and two other members of her team sat watching the video monitors as the British Airways flight from Istanbul disembarked, and a call came through from the Customs official standing outside the aircraft doors advising them of what Daniel was wearing. They would keep track of him on video from now on.

They caught sight of him standing on a moving walkway, and watched as he passed through Immigration. They had specifically requested that BA use the luggage carousel closest to Customs for this flight, though Daniel's luggage would be inspected before it ever reached it. Gill gave instructions to the uniformed staff on the ground, and they watched as Daniel progressed through the airport. Gill noted how uncomfortable he looked.

"A man with something on his mind if ever I saw one." she remarked.

***

Daniel followed the path for EU passport holders and stood patiently in the queue, which had been progressing quite quickly. When he reached the desk, he became convinced that they were taking a far longer look at his passport than any of the others, but the officer merely handed it back to him with a smile and looked at the next person in the queue. Relieved, Daniel glanced at the television monitor advising him which carousel would carry the luggage from his flight, then made his way down the escalators to the baggage reclaim hall.

He was one of the last to arrive, but soon found a gap in the waiting crowd, where he patiently watched for his suitcase. After a couple of minutes, the carousel started to rotate and the first cases began to appear. About fifteen minutes passed without any sign of his case, and Daniel was beginning to get worried. There were now only four cases doing a continual loop round the conveyor, and all but a few people had retrieved their luggage and gone on their way. He stood with his hand luggage between his feet and looked around him.

A tall, grey-haired Customs officer stood at the entrance of the 'nothing to declare' zone. He looked straight ahead to where Daniel was standing. Daniel averted his gaze and waited for another five minutes, during which time a few more bags appeared and disappeared. He was totally alone and on the verge of going to lost property when he saw his case come through the rubber curtain at the beginning of the belt. He sighed with relief, retrieved it and made his way towards the 'nothing to declare' zone. Once there, Daniel was surprised to note there were no other Customs officers in sight. His mood immediately lifted, but it was short lived. The officer who had been standing outside the zone had followed him in.

The next thing Daniel knew was an authoritative voice close behind him. "Excuse me sir, would you mind stepping over here for a minute." It was an order, not a question.

Daniel turned round with a start, feeling all the colour drain from his face. He stared at the officer for a moment that seemed like an eternity.

"Over here please, sir," the officer said, gesturing toward one of the tables.

Daniel said nothing, and almost as if in a trance wandered over to one of the tables to one side.

"Where have you just travelled from, sir?"

Daniel looked at the officer blankly while his mind tried to make sense of the situation. What a bloody stupid question that was! He had seen Daniel standing at the Istanbul carousel for the last half an hour.

"Where have you just come from, sir?" the officer repeated, this time with noticeably less politeness.

Daniel was so worried about the situation in hand that he found his voice box and jaws simply would not work.

"You do speak English, don't you sir?"

Daniel, realising how stupid he looked, finally managed to croak a response.

"Istanbul."

"I'm sorry sir, I didn't catch that, what did you say?"

"Istanbul," Daniel managed to say with a little more gusto.

"Would you mind putting your cases up on the table please, sir?"

Daniel obediently put his hand luggage on the table, and then heaved his suitcase up as well.

"Did you pack your suitcase yourself sir?"

"Er...yes, yes I did."

"Was it out of your sight at any time between you packing the case and checking it in at the airport?"

"Well, it was locked in the boot of the car while I did some sightseeing this morning, but apart from that, not at all."

"Are you carrying anything for anybody other than yourself?"

"I have are some sweets that were given to me by my hosts in Turkey."

"And what was the purpose of your visit to Istanbul?"

"I am in the marine industry, and we were looking at a factory in Turkey that may possibly be able to make some products for us."

"I see. I trust it was a successful trip, sir?"

"I hope so, but time will tell on that one."

To Daniel's surprise, the Customs officer did not ask him to open his case, but simply said, "Have a good onward journey. I'm sorry for the inconvenience."

Daniel collected his luggage from the table without saying a further word, and continued to where throngs of people waited. He felt dizzy with relief, and it was almost as much as he could do to stay upright without his legs collapsing from underneath him. He made his way on the underground walkway to the bus terminal, where he would get the airport link bus to Gatwick, and a taxi home from there. He was suddenly overcome with tiredness, and could not wait to get home to bed.

***

As Gill Bordeman stared at the monitor, the phone on the desk in front of her rang. It was Bill, the customs officer who had inspected Daniel's case before it had been released onto the belt.

"It's completely clean, only contained a couple of packets of confectionery which were all in order."

"Thank you Bill, we'll take it from here." She replaced the receiver.

"He's clean," she repeated to the others sitting around her, "Let's use standard monitoring, I don't think there's any need for surveillance. He's fairly predictable and has a family to look after. Get the guys down there to ask him what the nature of his business was in Turkey, and let's see what story comes back. He's probably completely legitimate."

Gill went over to another desk, picked up the phone to Grant, and updated him on the situation.

***

Daniel arrived home not long before midnight to see the house welcomingly lit up. Luke was obviously in, and Daniel started to wake up at the thought of all the information the two of them had to share. He was dying to know how things had gone in the US, along with Luke's view of the stupid suspicions that had made his life a misery over the last few days.

Daniel's keys were in his case, so he rang the front doorbell and waited. Luke eventually appeared, having clearly fallen asleep on the sofa waiting for Daniel's return. He put two more logs on the dwindling fire as Daniel poured them both a whisky.

They collapsed into the leather armchairs and Luke, unable to contain himself any longer, asked, "So how did it go, what were the boats like?"

Daniel paused. "In a nutshell, the boats were lousy and so was the whole trip. It's a long story, so why don't you tell me how you got on first?"

Luke started to tell Daniel about his trip, producing a brochure and a dealer manual with detailed product and accessory pricing that they both pored over until the early hours. After fighting to stay awake, they decided to continue their conversation the next day.

As Daniel trudged up to bed he knew that they would certainly go with the American factory. There was no comparison, and at that moment he didn't care if he never heard the word 'Turkey' again.

CHAPTER 36

The following morning, Daniel was the first to wake at about 10.30. He went downstairs to make a couple of cups of tea, then knocked on Luke's door. Luke was apparently still dead to the world, but he opened an eye and made a grunting noise Daniel took to be a thank you as he set a mug down.

About an hour later, Daniel prepared a cooked breakfast made up of all the leftovers that needed using before their departure for Singapore that evening. Luke appeared about ten minutes later, and they started to discuss all that needed doing upon their return. Luke made notes in his diary between mouthfuls, and Daniel made it clear to him that he thought the American factory was the only one worth entertaining. He promised to tell Luke all about his trip either on the plane or while they were waiting at the departure lounge, but gave him a quick idea of what the quality of the boats was like.

"The last thing we need to do is get involved with that sort of shit," agreed Luke.

They spent the early afternoon packing, although it would only be three or four weeks before one of them was back again. At one o'clock, they phoned their wives to let them know their ETA in Singapore, but as usual Vera had beaten them to it. Once all was taken care of, they headed into the office for a few hours to ensure that everything was under control. With email and fax, it was decided, there was very little they couldn't manage from the Singapore office simply by monitoring the daily reports the London team had agreed to send over in Gordon's absence.

Once they had navigated the airport, Daniel and Luke sat in economy class seats by one of the fire exits with a glass of red wine, and Daniel proceeded to tell Luke what had happened during the trip to Istanbul. He left nothing out, but Luke was convinced that all Daniel's worries had been in his mind.

"I'd have told you not be so bloody stupid if you had phoned me!" he said. "But there were so many things that didn't make sense! It's not as if it was just one isolated incident; something new always backed up my suspicions."

"Sounds like the onset of paranoia, if you ask me." Luke said drily.

"Well, I can assure you that if you had been there, you'd have probably felt very differently." Daniel said sharply. He had known from the outset that there would be no sympathy from Luke.

They both sat and browsed the in-flight magazine until dinner arrived. Over their meals, they started to discuss the next steps for the UK company, and what needed to be addressed in the next visit. The subject of Istanbul did not come up again—they both knew that the option of building boats in Turkey had been consigned to history, and they would now put all their efforts into moving forward with the American factory.

***

As Daniel and Luke walked down the steps to the baggage claim at Changi Airport, they could see their families waving at them furiously with beaming smiles on their faces. Daniel and Luke waved back and wandered towards the conveyor. Their cases were among the first off the aircraft, and before long there were hugs and kisses all round.

The girls had driven to the airport in one car, so they had to divert via Luke and Michelle's house to drop them off. Luke and Daniel remained fairly quiet as Michelle and Linda tried to bring them both up to date with the gossip in Singapore. There would be plenty of time to tell their stories later.

After Sam was in bed, Linda and Daniel collapsed into the rattan chairs on the veranda with large gin and tonics loaded with ice. Daniel inquired as to what had happened with Salvia, and Linda told him the whole story.

"She has taken her stuff and gone, thank goodness," she concluded. "We'll get an advert put in for another *amah* this week, and put that chapter behind us."

When she was finished, Daniel proceeded to tell Linda all about his trip to Istanbul, again leaving out no detail.

Linda, knowing Daniel's uncanny perception of people and situations, did not take the issue nearly as lightly as Luke had, and genuinely felt that Han had probably been sizing Daniel up for a role in some sort of illegitimate business.

"I think it's a very good job you stuck to your guns and didn't go out gallivanting with him," she said. "Who knows where you could have ended up? It sounds to me as if you had a fairly close shave, but what I don't understand is Lim's role. Perhaps he felt he could earn a buck or two by recruiting you?"

"You might be right, but there are still several things that don't make sense. Anyway, I guess we will never know, as it is certainly nothing Luke or I intend to follow up on. I think we're best out of it."

"You most certainly are. In any case, the American deal makes much more sense, and maybe I'll get my trip to Disney World with Sam," Linda smiled. "Perhaps when you and Luke go out to sign the contract we could all make a couple of weeks of it."

"Steady, honey. It'd be more like a week, but that's not a bad idea."

Within an hour they were in bed, but despite their fatigue, sleep was on neither of their minds. They had some serious catching up to do, and tension to relieve.

***

Daniel arrived in the office before seven o'clock the following morning and was surprised to find that Luke was there already. They both spent the next couple of hours going through the mounds of post Vera had left on their desks. She had looked after all the urgent mail and inquiries during their absence, leaving them only what would wait. She really was an angel of efficiency; worth every penny they paid her.

They decided to fax the factory in Georgia to confirm their interest in becoming the sole agents for their products in the UK, and copied all relevant information to the UK office, asking for any thoughts they may have on the subject. It was decided they would shoot a fax off to Han stating that they were not interested in the products the Turkish factory had to offer, but thanking them for their hospitality. This letter would also be copied to Lim at the Singapore office.

Vera arrived in the office at bang on nine o'clock, as always, and Luke presented her with a box of Scottish Highland shortbread and some Russell and Bromley soaps that Linda and Michelle had bought during their trip to London. Every time either of them went away, they always tried to buy a little something for Vera to show her that she was appreciated.

At about 9.30, Linda rang to remind Daniel to place the advert for the *amah*. She had not seen her husband that morning; he had been up and out of the house well before she had woken.

"Vera, did you hear about the frightening time Linda had during my absence?" he said after hanging up.

"Yes, Linda spoke to me about it. It was most unfortunate, and undoubtedly very frightening for her, but she handled it impeccably. I have been asking around, and I know of a very good *amah*. She is currently working for some Chinese friends of mine, but will be looking for new employment when my they go to work in Hong Kong next month."

"What's she like?" Daniel enquired.

"She is a traditional Chinese *amah*, very clean and a good cook."

"Have you mentioned her to Linda?"

"No, I thought I would wait until you got back, and discuss it with you before interfering."

"Well, I have no hesitation in asking if could you arrange a meeting for us. In fact, I will ring Linda back right now."

The meeting was arranged for the following morning; and when it came, Daniel and Linda were pleased to find that the new *amah* was everything they were looking for, and more. Her current employers had written a glowing reference, and stated that they would not hesitate to recommend her to any future employer. She would start as soon as her other employers left Singapore in about four weeks' time.

***

For the next few weeks their lives returned to a routine, into the office at nine, home at five. Daniel and Linda got back into the social swing of things, and frequently had to utilise their newfound babysitter, who was grateful for the money. Curiously enough, neither Luke nor Daniel came across Lim in the Tanglin Club, despite going there a great number of times, and there had been no response to the faxes, so they assumed the Turks had simply let the whole lot drop.

***

It was four weeks later as they were planning the next trip to London and the United States trip with their families that the phone rang in the office. To the surprise of both of them, Vera announced that it was Lim.

Luke looked at Daniel quizzically.

"I'll take it," said Daniel, picking up the phone on his desk. "Edward, hi. How's it going?"

"Fine, thank you Daniel. How are things with you?"

"Not too bad, but very busy. Anyhow, to what do we owe this pleasure?"

"I am just phoning to let you know that I have received word from Han. The first four boats are on the way to your company in England, and he has asked me to assure you that they are all from the new moulds. You will be very pleased with them, we're sure."

Daniel was speechless for several moments before responding.

"But Edward, you must have received our fax? We specifically said that we were not interested. Following the unsatisfactory state of the boats, we have signed with another factory. I'm sorry, but your product does not fit in with our M.O."

"What fax are you talking about?"

"We faxed you shortly after arriving back in Singapore. We also faxed Han with the same information."

"Well, we never received the faxes. We can discuss terms later."

"Edward, I'm sorry to be abrupt, but there are no terms to discuss. We're simply unable to do business with you."

"This is very bad news; very, very bad news." he said gravely. "Well, if you just look after the boats for a while, we will arrange to take them away."

"Edward, are you in your office at the moment?"

"Yes."

"Let me talk to Luke. We have made a decision, and we do not have room to store excess stock, but leave it with me."

"OK, I will talk with you later."

Daniel replaced the receiver and stared at Luke in disbelief.

"What's up?" asked Luke.

"They've only got four bloody boats on the way to us. They say they didn't get our faxes."

"They can't do that!"

"They just have, and they want us to take them in until they can remove them. I'll phone him back right now and inform him that under no circumstances can we take any responsibility for the boats, and that they'll either have to find someone else in the UK or turn them round on the docks and ship them back. Vera, could you write a letter to the same tune and post it, as well faxing a copy to Han in Istanbul?"

"Sure." She turned round and started tapping away on her computer keyboard, while Daniel picked up the phone and dialled Lim's office.

"Hello?"

"Edward, it's Daniel. I have spoken to Luke, and we agree you will have to find someone else to take the boats in. I'm sorry, but we cannot help on this one."

"They are on the way, and all the documentation is filled out as coming to you. Can you just take delivery before we arrange to collect?"

"No, we cannot. We are not prepared to import boats that are without CE ratings or certificates."

"We will pay you well for your inconvenience."

"It's not about money, I can assure you. I am truly sorry, but we are going to be unable to help."

"OK I will talk with Han." Lim hung up, and Daniel was left looking at the receiver.

"I think he's pissed off," Daniel announced as he replaced the handset in its cradle. "I had better go down and see him later in the week. After all, it's better not to fall out with these people."

"Business is business." Luke responded. "Who cares?"

Daniel let the last comment drop as Vera handed him the completed letter for approval and signature.

He could not help but think that they had not heard the last of Edward Lim.

CHAPTER 37

Han had only spoken with Lim three or four times since the trip out on the Ferretti, and that was to advise him of progress.

The boats were now in the build phase, and would be ready for shipping on schedule. He now waited for word from Lim, who was to call once he had spoken with Daniel or Luke. They had both received the fax from Daniel stating they were not interested, but they had decided to see if they could at least get the first two boats into the UK care of the British company.

The phone on Han's desk rang, and he jumped to answer it.

"They are definitely not going to play ball. If we send the boats to them, they will end up sitting on the docks and we will be unable to move them. You will have to talk to Eugene and use plan two."

"OK, I will get everything moving."

"Let me know the schedule when you have it. I'll meet you in London. I'm pulling out of Singapore tomorrow, there is no further need to stay."

Han replaced the receiver and immediately picked it up again to phone Eugene.

"As I expected," said Eugene. "I have already started making some room in my yard. They will be out of sight from the road behind the yard gates. I have also set up a company called Marinetrade Ltd. I know it has no history, but it might give some more credibility when importing than two boats coming to an individual."

"Good, please send me all the details for the shipping documents," said Han. "I will arrive in about three weeks, and we can make the final preparations. Do you still have your Landcruiser?"

"Yes of course."

"Good, we will need that, and a vehicle to tow the boats from the docks. Can you arrange that?"

"Leave it with me. Just let me know when you arrive, and I will collect you at Heathrow."

CHAPTER 38

Daniel found Linda spring-cleaning the *amah*'s quarters, which Salvia had left in a mess. She was dripping with perspiration and filthy, but she had done a fine job.

"Why don't you go and change?" she said. "By the time you're done, I'll be in to have a shower."

"OK honey. How was Sam today?"

"He's been asking about Disney World again."

"t's all arranged, we will be going in three weeks' time. I'll spare you the details until you've got a drink in your hand."

He made his way back into the house and went upstairs to shower and change into some shorts and a T-shirt before pouring them both a gin and tonic.

"A picture of contentment," Linda smiled as she joined him on the veranda.

"Unfortunately, the picture is deceptive," Daniel answered as his wife sank down next to him.

"Why do you say that?"

"Edward Lim was on the phone again today, and I can't help feeling we haven't heard the last of him."

He told her about the conversation with Lim. Linda listened carefully, as she always did, before she passed comment. When he had finished, the sun had slipped behind the trees and darkness was falling. Linda got up to switch the veranda lights on.

"If you have told him you will not accept any responsibility for the boats if they arrive in the UK, I'm sure he will heed that," she said. "After all, it will cost *him* money if they sit at the dockside with delays or have to be returned. Just make sure you have copies of the faxes sent to him with the time and date of transmission in case there are any queries, though I don't see how there could be."

Daniel pulled her close and gave her a kiss on the forehead. "I'm sure you're right honey, I'll try and forget about it."

"Tell me what you have arranged for the States," she said, settling into her seat again.

"Well, we're off the Friday after next. We fly into California, travel to Jacksonville, then go straight to Georgia for two nights, where we are meeting Bob Johnson from the UK office at the boat factory. After he flies back to the UK, the five of us are off to Orlando for a week. We'll then go back to the UK for two weeks, then home. What do you think?"

"It'll be a wonderful trip. I can't wait!" She turned and gave him a big hug, almost spilling both their drinks.

"Steady, honey, steady. You really are worse than Sam!"

Linda smiled sheepishly as she stood. "I'll go and put the pizzas in. Thank goodness Sue Lee starts in the morning."

"Yes, she will be a godsend. What time are we expecting her?"

"I told her to come at around elevenish."

***

The following morning, Daniel decided to stay at home to greet Sue Lee with Linda, which would give him a chance to spend the morning with Sam. He had had too little time with him in the past few months, and was missing watching him grow.

When Sam came in and woke them at eight o'clock, Daniel got up and went to make he and Linda a cup of tea. They all went for a swim before breakfast, and while Daniel washed up, Linda tidied the house, making sure it was in the presentable state they expected it to be kept.

Sue Lee arrived at eleven o'clock sharp, and Daniel carried her luggage from the taxi to her quarters for her, much to her embarrassment. They sat down to discuss timetables for meals, the dog's diet, and Sam's needs. It was clear that Sue Lee was going to run a tight ship.

***

Two days before they were due to leave for the US, Daniel was on his way home from the office when he decided to pay Lim a visit. When he arrived at the offices of United European Marine Ltd, the door was locked, so Daniel rang the intercom. There was no answer, but he tried once more. As he rang the second time, a door opposite banged shut and there came the rustling of keys as a secretary locked up for the evening. When she saw Daniel, she called, "Nobody there any more."

"I'm sorry, what do you mean?"

"They closed up about a week ago, move out. My boss say he not pay any rent since he arrive."

"Oh. Thank you."

Daniel tried to add this latest piece of information to the jigsaw in his mind as he made his way back down to the car park. He would try calling Lim's office to see if there was an answering machine message, he decided. If nothing else, it would satisfy his curiosity.

CHAPTER 39

Two days later, they were all aboard a Singapore Airlines 747 400 jet eastbound for California via Hong Kong. They would spend one night in Bel Air to break up the journey before catching an onward flight to Jacksonville the following day.

The hotel in Bel Air was one Daniel had visited many years before with his parents. While not the most expensive, it was delightful, with a fine pool and a good restaurant all set among pleasant gardens.

They arrived by late afternoon, all very tired. Sam was the only one who did not appear to be suffering too much, partly through having slept on the aircraft, but more due to the prospect of Disney World. As they were checking in, the question "Is this where Pooh Bear lives?" could be heard for the umpteenth time. They all agreed a swim was in order after dropping off their bags, followed by a drink at the pool bar, a quick meal, and an early night.

***

Later that evening, the sun was beginning to set in the deep blue sky over Los Angeles, and the landscaped gardens were bathed in light.

"I wish we were spending the entire break here," said Michelle. "It's paradise, and Disneyland is only around the corner."

"It's not all play," said Luke. "We've got work to do in Georgia, which is the whole excuse for the trip."

"How silly of me to forget!" Michelle responded sarcastically, catching Linda's eye. Daniel noticed this, but decided not to ask.

By the time they had finished dinner, they were all ready for bed. Sam was the first to disturb the peace after only four and a half hours when he decided he was hungry. Daniel gave Sam some Weetabix they had brought with them, quickly deciding to join him. Within minutes, so did Linda. They switched on the television and ended up watching a re-run of I Love Lucy, but were all back to sleep within the hour.

***

They arrived in Jacksonville having spent another entire day travelling. There was still the journey to Waycross, but they were all exhausted, and decided they would meet Bob Johnson here instead. in Jacksonville. He could join them all for the drive the next day. They picked up a rental Chrysler Voyager, and drove to the nearest Days Inn. After checking in, they found a local Wal-Mart, where they stocked up on all they would require for the journey and series of motel room stays over the next week.

***

Bob Johnson was as surprised as anyone when he saw the entourage waiting for him at Jacksonville airport the following morning, but he was relieved. The mere thought of going to the States and having to find his way around had given him sleepless nights, but now he could just tag along.

Daniel sat in the back of the Chrysler with Sam, while Luke, who had made the journey before, drove the few hours north to the factory and fielded Bob's questions about it. The girls nattered quietly, and rest of the drive passed comfortably and without a hitch.

***

They checked into the hotel in Waycross, and the men headed off to the factory to start discussing the finer points of the deal. Both Bob and Daniel were awed by the immense scale of production and delighted with the new products on display. The more Daniel saw, the more he realised they had definitely made the right choice.

The heat was extreme, and after walking round the factory for some thirty minutes, they all welcomed the idea of returning to the air-conditioned meeting room for an ice-cold Coca Cola to resume talks. As they spoke, Daniel was immensely reassured by the whole trading ethic of the US company. They wanted paying for the product before it left their shores, and parts inventories were discussed along with marketing budgets and support. There were certainly no oddities or suspicions here.

They spent the rest of the day at the factory, asking relevant questions and gleaning advice for the forthcoming partnership between their businesses.

Once satisfied, they headed back to the motel at about 6pm, and the whole party visited a steakhouse that Luke had found on his last visit, but by 9pm they were all sound asleep.

***

The Oakleys and Cassidys drove back to Jacksonville to drop Bob at the airport early the following morning, then went for a day at Daytona Beach. While Sam enjoyed the sand, the others chatted and sunbathed. They left at about 4pm to check into the Howard Johnson, where they would stay until their flight home. The girls were happy to be able to unpack clothes and hang them up, knowing they were staying for a while.

***

The hotel ran a shuttle bus to the main gate of Disneyworld, and they were all on board the first one to leave the next morning. It wasn't just Sam who enjoyed the first day, and they were thoroughly relaxed by the time they sat around the pool that evening. The following week passed in a blur, with visits to Epcot, Universal Studios, the Kennedy Space Centre, and Florida Mall. They all agreed that they needed three times as long to enjoy Florida properly in the future.

CHAPTER 40

Daniel and Luke spent the following week at the UK office preparing the staff for the new products that were due to arrive from America, as well as trying to smooth things over with one of the Singapore customers who was not happy a forty foot container had arrived with everything inside damaged. It had taken all of Daniel's diplomacy to calm the customer down, as they would lose a number of weeks' sales before replacements could be manufactured and brought in. On further investigation, it transpired that the shipping line had actually dropped the container from a crane on the docks, so they would pick up the tab for replacing everything, much to Daniel and Luke's relief.

They left the office early on Friday to travel to Dorset with the girls and Sam, where they were due to spend the weekend with Daniel's parents, before flying back to Singapore on the Monday. Over a leisurely Saturday breakfast, they laughed and joked. After a while, Daniel's mother went to brew more tea, and returned from the kitchen with a worried frown to ask if they had seen the news.

"No, why do you ask?"

"There was quite a bit about boats."

"Oh, really?" asked Linda.

***

CHAPTER 41

Grant, Gill and the team at HM Customs had realised that there had been no contact between Daniel Cassidy and Han for the past few weeks. Having monitored his movements and tapped into the phone lines, they were now fairly sure that he didn't have anything to do with the suspected drugs deal.

The Singapore authorities advised Gill that there had been one or two faxes to Turkey initially, but these had been intercepted and read. They had indicated that relationship was clearly an honest one, at least from Daniel's side. Of more concern was the identity of a Mr Edward Lim, for whom they could find no background information. They had kept an eye on his office after his phone calls to Daniel, but had found no movement. A week later, after they had let themselves in and found it deserted, their suspicions became even more aroused. Daniel Cassidy was currently out of town, but they wanted to talk to him when he returned to see if he could help solve this mystery.

Meanwhile, the British authorities were convinced that Han was up to no good, but no proof had yet been forthcoming, at least not until they had a message from

Turkish authorities advising them that two boats were being shipped by one of Han's companies to a company called Marinetrade Ltd, based in London. The boats would be inspected before leaving Turkey aboard the *Pan Ultima* in two days' time.

***

Han had been extremely good at covering his tracks in Turkey, and had spent a lot of time in Israel while things were put together at the factory. He had only made contact with the managing director from untraceable public phones on Lim's advice, and would not see the boats until they were delivered to their new owners in the UK.

They had been towed to the docks on their own trailers by two separate vehicles, both fitted with false plates and driven by his acquaintances. The paperwork was sealed in envelopes, and all they had to do was drop the boats off at the docks and leave.

It was while this paperwork was being processed that warning bells rang in the shipping company's office. They had received a list from Customs, and had been told that if any name on it appeared on any paperwork they handled, they were to be informed immediately. The shipping company obliged, and Customs hauled the boats to one of their sheds to examine them and deploy sniffer dogs, but touched nothing. Their observations were forwarded to London.

The boats were cleared from the Turkish side and duly loaded into the belly of the *Pan Ultima*. Gill and Grant would have a team standing by to do a closer inspection when the boats arrived at Southampton.

A week before the arrival of the *Pan Ultima*, Grant's phone rang.

"Grant, it's Gill. There's an interesting scenario developing."

"What do you mean?"

"Guess who has just arrived on a flight from the US into Heathrow?"

"Han, I would think, but that would be no great surprise."

"Our friend Daniel Cassidy.".

"Well, that *is* a coincidence—what timing!"

"Exactly. Maybe our hunch was wrong, and Daniel has been cleverer than we think in all this. He's got his whole family in tow, and he's here with his business partner."

"We'd better see what they're up to; make sure we know where they are at all times. By the way, what's the word on Han?"

"He was last seen boarding a flight to Israel, but we're monitoring all likely entry points. He's bound to show eventually, I'll keep you informed."

"I've asked the boys at Southampton to tow the boats to one of our sheds immediately they are offloaded. We'll head down first thing Friday morning, if you're happy with that?"

"Sounds good to me."

Three and a half hours later, Gill rang Grant again.

"Grant, he's just flown into Luton. He seems to be heading to London, possibly to see Eugene of Marinetrade Ltd."

"Well that would make sense. Two arrivals in one day, it's certainly all happening. Who's on that surveillance?"

"Mike and Helen are on that one at the moment."

"Good. Allocate all the resources you need, I'll catch up with you later."

Gill set about making the necessary arrangements for the arrival of the boats, which they were quite sure contained some sort of illegitimate substance. They had already informed the Metropolitan Police that their assistance would probably be needed if they did.

***

Mike and Helen followed Han in his rented Nissan to Eugene's car yard. They had already tapped into his mobile frequency, but as yet had heard nothing untoward. Most of the phone calls appeared to be from various women he was seeing, ranging from new relationships to those he was trying to get rid of. Nothing was said about the boats.

However, while Eugene had been equally careful to limit discussions about them with Han, he was not so cautious with others, and it was soon apparent that the boats were due to be towed back on Friday, with money changing hands that evening.

***

Grant and Gill gave the operation their undivided attention. That Friday morning, as they headed down the M3 from London to Southampton, they felt adrenaline start to flow in anticipation of what they had in store that day. They had ten undercover operatives on the case, as well as the Met standing by for the anticipated bust. As they drove, the boats were being taken into the Customs shed. Grant glanced at the clock on the dashboard and pressed the accelerator a bit harder.

***

The latest news was that Daniel and Luke had done nothing of interest at all in the week prior to the boats' arrival, and Paul, who had been assigned to keep tabs on them, was bored. He felt he was missing out on the action, but smiled as he remembered how a colleague had once described the job—"hours of boredom, punctuated by moments of panic, followed by months of paperwork". *How very true*, he thought, but he knew he would not change his job for the world.

Based on the telephone conversations he had been monitoring, the group were all heading to visit Daniel's parents that weekend, so Gill decided to call him off, and told him to get himself to London. Relieved, Paul had the engine running and the car rolling almost before Gill had finished giving the instruction.

***

Grant and Gill arrived at the docks at 11am, and had just walked in when one of the Customs officers put his phone call on hold and leaned towards them.

"I've got the shipping agents on the phone, they want to know if the boats have been cleared yet. They've apparently got the customer on the line wanting to know when he can collect them."

Grant's response was swift. "Tell them they will be cleared and ready for collection by 3pm. Make sure the shipping company stresses that there is no problem and the boats are going through fast track clearance."

This message was relayed back to the shipping agents, and ultimately on to Han and Eugene, who were standing by with two 4x4s to head down to Southampton to collect the boats.

Grant, Gill, the local divisional boss, and three other officers headed down to the shed, where two springer spaniels and their handlers waited patiently for them.

"The Turkish authorities reckon there is something in the bow of both boats, but they have not been inside to investigate what," said Grant.

"I should say there is," said one of the handlers, "Poppy here is going mad, and she's not been within ten feet of it yet."

"OK then," nodded Grant. "Let's get on with it."

Poppy's handler sent her into the cockpit of the boat and gradually worked her forwards, ensuring that she investigated every locker and compartment. As she approached the bow, she started to whine and whimper, her tail wagging like mad. They removed the seat cushions in the area of interest, but there were no lockers or compartments to be found. She scrabbled at the surface of the fibreglass frantically.

"OK, cut it open, but in a way that we can patch it back up again before collection this afternoon. I don't want him to know we've been here."

One of the officers came in with a small jigsaw and started to cut the hull open in along its natural ridge. Conscious of the dogs and lacking the proper protection, the others waited outside while the fibreglass was being cut. After a few minutes, they heard the saw stop, and then a shout.

"Fucking hell, you lot won't believe this!"

Grant was the first to clamber back up onto the boat. He peered into the small hole that had been cut.

"Jesus Christ, this is unreal!"

Stuffed inside the hull were a number of plastic bags. Grant made a small slit in one of them and brought a tiny amount of the substance inside out on the end of his knife.

"Well, chaps and chapesses, we've got ourselves a whole lot of top grade heroin by the looks of it," he said. "The next step is to see where it's going. Patch this back up, and we'd better make bloody sure we don't lose sight of it. Are we equipped if the boats go in different directions?"

"Yes, it's all covered," replied Gill. "I don't think there are any eventualities I've missed."

"Good, get on to the Met and let them know we definitely will need their assistance tonight. Tell them to give it top priority, I don't want any of their usual excuses about manpower."

"Will do. If both of these contain the same amount, there must be upward of thirty million pounds' worth here."

Everyone stood silently for a few moments. This was much, much bigger than any of them had dared imagine. It was going to be one of the largest drugs hauls ever recorded in the UK.

They all wandered up to the offices, still focused. They would wait to celebrate after they had captured the people responsible, as they knew it was far from over yet.

Grant got straight onto the Turkish authorities, who had requested to be kept up to date with the situation. They were keen to get to the source, but still had no idea where the boats originated.

The hole was patched up so that it would only be noticeable on close inspection, after removing some carpet. It was allowed to dry for half an hour before the seats were put back in, and the boats were then towed back to the storage yard to await collection.

***

Paul's phone rang as he drove towards London.

"Paul, it's Grant. Listen, I want you to get straight up to Eugene's yard; we're fairly sure that's where they are gonna be heading. Find vantage points that overlook it, and set up video. I also want you to liaise with the Met. This is far bigger than any of us expected, there must be upward of thirty million quid's worth of heroin here."

"Bloody hell! That's one of the biggest hauls in history."

"Exactly. That's why I don't want any screw-ups."

Paul had said his goodbyes and drove with a renewed sense of urgency, taking his Omega up to 95 miles an hour, but keeping an eye open for traffic squads. He couldn't be bothered with the aggro of being stopped right now; it would only delay him.

***

Paul met up with Mike and Helen a couple of streets away from Eugene's yard. They had been keeping an eye on the movements of both Han and Eugene, and updated Paul on with the geography of the yard and offices, mentioning that they had witnessed new gates being put up a couple of days prior, blocking whatever would be behind them from view. Fortunately, they had noticed there was a bathroom in one of the adjoining houses overlooking the yard.

A young mother answered the door with a baby in her arms, and the sound of a toddler could be heard from the back of the house. Paul explained that they were carrying out some routine surveillance in the area, and that they would like to use the room with the east-facing window. After some close examination of his ID, she reluctantly agreed.

The bathroom in question was cramped, with a toilet fixed right under the mottled glass window. It offered no proper visibility, and to Paul's disappointment, the only part of the window he could use was the unfrosted quarter window at the top. He clambered onto the toilet to see what view it afforded. To his relief, it was perfect.

The next problem was the tripods for both the video and still cameras. It took him at least an hour to get them into the right position, but when he'd finished, he had complete coverage of the yard. He could watch what was going on from a remote screen, and the window only needed opening a notch to allow full vision.

There was still no movement in the yard, but as he got outside, Mike and Helen informed him they had just heard from Gill. Apparently, the two vehicles had just arrived at the docks for the collection. Han and Eugene were currently with the shipping agents doing the paperwork, and would probably be back in London within a couple of hours, so they needed to take their places around the yard in case anyone arrived early to collect the goods.

***

Gill and Grant planned to follow the shipment, supported initially by some plain-clothes officers from the Hampshire constabulary. This duty would then be handed over to the Metropolitan Police, who would take up the operation from the Fleet motorway services London-bound. Meanwhile, Gill and Grant would move to a service station outside the docks to pick the boats' movements up from there. They would be visible on the Customs surveillance cameras until that point, so if there was an unexpected change of route, Gill and Grant would be informed by the officers monitoring them.

***

Once the paperwork was complete, Eugene and Han exited the docks in exactly the anticipated direction. Before long, they were on the M27, and heading north on the M3. Grant and Gill followed at a safe distance while two other Hampshire cars tailed them. Grant was happy for the moment, and phoned Paul to update him.

Immediately after putting the phone down to Paul, Grant's mobile rang again. It was head office, who had been monitoring all conversations on both Eugene's and Han's mobiles. Han seemed to think he was home and dry, because he had finally made a call in connection with the boats. It was to a Singapore mobile number, but had been answered in London by a man calling himself Edward. The message exchanged was that everything was on schedule and that the goods would be collected on Saturday morning as arranged.

"OK, thank you for that," Grant nodded. "Can you get onto the Singapore authorities and see if you can find out more on that number? It sounds like our friend Mr Lim has surfaced."

Grant immediately phoned Paul, brought him up to date once more, and asked him to brief the others, as well as the police. None of them would be getting much sleep that night.

***

Han and Eugene trudged up the M3 at an unusually sedate 50 miles per hour. They were not going to get stopped for speeding and blow it all at the last hurdle. As they approached Fleet Services, they both pulled off. Alarm bells started ringing in the minds of the agents following them, though their fears of a rearranged drop were alleviated when Han and Eugene bought burgers and ate them in the car before continuing on their way.

The remainder of the journey was relatively uneventful, and London was not too congested, though it was not too difficult to tail a couple of large, slow-moving boats in any case.

The pair blocked the traffic for a couple of minutes as Eugene got out to unlock the new gates, then swung them open and pulled his vehicle in. The yard was not enormous, and the arrival of two large boats and their tow vehicles certainly dominated things. Eugene had mere inches to close the gates behind them.

Mike, Helen, Paul, Grant, Gill, and three unmarked police cars each containing three specially trained officers all took up their positions. Paul would be their eyes and ears inside, as the others could only monitor those arriving or leaving, which they did not expect to happen that evening. The two men would be too nervous about leaving such valuable cargo unattended.

They all readied themselves for a long night, one person at each vantage point staying awake to keep watch. Another colleague, Tim, joined Paul at about 11pm, much to the disapproval of the homeowner, who by now just wanted her bathroom back.

All was quiet until six minutes past eight the following morning, when Grant's mobile rang. It was Alan from the office.

"Grant, listen, I'm phoning from home. It's all over the news this morning."

"What on earth are you talking about?"

"The boats, the drugs; the BBC even have pictures of the exact models."

Grant jumped to his feet. "Shit, you can't be serious! Get straight onto them, it's got to be blanked immediately or it will blow the whole thing apart, if it hasn't already. Call as many outlets as you can and ring me back to confirm."

Grant hung up and dialled Paul's number, briefly explaining things to Gill as he did. Gill, who had been dozing in the back of the car, was jolted wide-awake by the news, and immediately rang the rest of the team as Grant spoke.

"Paul, it's Grant. Is there any movement in there, is anything being said?"

"No, it would appear they are asleep still."

"Good, but I fear the contact may not show. It's been all over the news this morning."

"How? Only we know!"

"Along with half the dockyard at Southampton. We're going to have to go in as soon as he tries to move the drugs or makes any attempt to leave. Keep me up to date, I'll warn the Met to be ready."

He closed his phone and swore as he chucked it into the footwell. "People and their fucking big mouths, it's a bloody nightmare! Gill, can you brief the police?"

"Yes, sure."

Gill contacted the officer in charge of the police operation as Grant sat in the driver's seat, hands covering his face. They sat in the car for a further hour, exchanging messages with their colleagues and the police. They were all nervous, and it was beginning to show.

At about 9.30 Han appeared in the yard, followed closely by Eugene. Paul started to click away on the still camera, simultaneously videoing their every move. The two men carried tools, which they placed in the cockpit of one of the boats. They unhitched one boat and moved the tow vehicle into an L-shaped section of the yard, then did the same with the second boat, pushing the boats into the void left by the tow vehicles. Han reversed the Discovery up to the back of the boats and opened the rear door.

"There is something going on, movement," Paul said into his radio. The others sat waiting, hardly daring to breathe in case they missed something. They knew it would not be much longer now, and would not be at ease until this was all over.

"Han is entering the right hand boat with tools—he has what looks like a jigsaw," said Paul over the radio. "Eugene is laying an extension lead out, I can't see what's going on inside the cabin."

"Couple of minutes," Gill replied quietly into her radio, addressing the waiting teams.

"Paul, when you have both video and still proof of them with the substance, we'll move," Grant said.

"OK. I can hear an electric saw, it won't be long now."

As Paul looked down, white dust started to appear from the cabin hatch. He stood on the toilet to look out of the quarter window, which was clearer than his screen. It appeared to be the glass fibre and gel coat being cut by the jigsaw. Paul sat back down to watch his monitor, while Tim clicked away with the still camera every time they came into view.

Eugene appeared at the hatch and jumped to the ground as Han clambered out into the cockpit carrying two bags. He handed them to Eugene, who placed them in the back of the Discovery. Han disappeared back into the boat, and the procedure was repeated. Paul relayed their movements to the teams.

Grant and Gill had decided to wait until the men in the yard had nearly finished offloading the second boat, which happened swiftly. Before they moved in, Paul confirmed that the whole process had been caught on film. There was no longer any doubt as to their intentions, and the evidence was irrefutable.

"Knock, Knock, Knock!"

Grant's words echoed through the radio system. Within seconds, a sea of navy blue surrounded the gate, and the police utilized a Range Rover as a battering ram. The gates gave little resistance, flying open as soon as its tow bar touched them. The car pulled forward sharply, and foot officers and Customs squads teemed into the small yard.

Han and Eugene both looked up, startled. Armed police surrounded Han immediately, but Eugene bolted towards the road. The first policeman to try and stop him was sent sprawling as Eugene hit him with enormous force, but after a small scuffle, he found himself hopelessly outnumbered by those at the gate. Han looked around helplessly as he was told to put his hands on his head and both men were read their rights.

***

Grant's team spent the rest of the day taking down details and photographing the evidence, along with its places of concealment. Grant and Gill were disappointed they hadn't had the chance to catch the recipient, but they had stopped an enormous amount of heroin hitting the streets. They would still celebrate that evening.

One of Grant's first calls as he got back to the office that afternoon was to thank the Turkish authorities, without whom the raid might never have happened. They confirmed they would do everything possible to find out where the drugs and boats had originated, and to stop the day's events reoccurring.

CHAPTER 42

Xu was up early; he was to do the money brokering with the customer at the yard later that morning. He had the television on in his hotel room, and nearly fell over in his haste to get out of the bathroom to hear what the news presenter was saying.

"Officers from HM Customs and Excise are in the process of intercepting a large drugs shipment at Southampton docks this morning. Early reports suggest as much as £30,000,000 worth of heroin was moulded into the front buoyancy tanks of two boats arriving from Turkey."

Two boats of the kind described were pictured, and Xu looked on in horror.

"We will keep you updated as further details emerge."

He froze, staring at the screen for a moment or two longer, before throwing clothes onto the bed. He was probably being watched at that moment, and had to get out.

He packed as quickly as he could, went straight to the underground car park and jumped into his rented Ford Focus, heading for Luton Airport. He would take the first flight out, and destroy his SIM card as soon as possible. Edward Lim would cease to exist.

***

Xu Xiang flew into Singapore's Changi Airport on a Lufthansa flight late the next day to pick up his car and drive back across the causeway into Malaysia. He was confident he had covered his tracks well, but of one thing he was sure; heads would roll over this loss.

CHAPTER 43

Linda and the others listened as Daniel's mother recounted the events on the earlier news broadcast.

"That was probably old Han!" said Daniel jokingly, not really believing it, but intrigued.

"If it was, we had a close call," said Linda seriously. She sensed that Daniel's comment was closer to the mark than they realised.

The following day they headed back to Sussex, and Daniel and Luke went into the office while the girls tidied and prepared for the journey back to Singapore. With the US boats lined up, everyone in the UK was looking forward to a good year.

The two families headed for Heathrow that evening with mixed emotions, and were simultaneously sorrowful at leaving and eagerly anticipating the warmth waiting for them the other end. They were not held up at Customs or Immigration despite Daniel's nerves, and were soon on their way.

***

In custody, Han said very little, offering no real leads. Eugene, on the other hand, told them everything he knew. For the most part, the information was not new, apart from the mention of a Mr Lim, Han's partner. This tallied with the Singapore mobile phone number Gill and Grant had discovered.

When questioned about Edward Lim, Han remained silent, adamant he would disclose nothing at this stage. It was becoming apparent that Gill and Grant would need to talk to Singaporean authorities at greater length, as well as interview the Cassidys, who Grant had been told had returned to Singapore that morning. They would leave in a week, sending Paul and Mike out to Istanbul to do some homework with the authorities there.

***

Once more, Daniel and Luke soon settled back into their routine. Vera had run the office in Beach Road with fastidious efficiency, and Sue Lee had kept the house immaculate, though Skipper was looking decidedly on the plump side.

Two weeks after their return, Daniel's stepsister and brother-in-law, Diana and Garth, arrived for a four-day stay in Singapore on the way back from Bali. Linda and Daniel had invited them to stay at the house, but Diana had insisted they stay at the Raffles Hotel.

Daniel collected Diana and Garth that evening for a dinner party Linda was preparing for the four of them, along with their neighbours John and Tara. They enjoyed aperitifs round the rattan bar in the sitting room before retiring to the dining room for the meal. It was the first time Daniel and Linda had seen Diana and Garth for quite a while, as well as their first opportunity to properly catch up with John and Tara. The conversation turned to Turkey, and Daniel ended up taking them all through the story piece by piece. They were all spellbound.

"Sounds like my worst nightmare," John said when Daniel had finished.

"Daniel, my God!" said Diana. "You could have been in jail now. It's an amazing story, but it could only have happened to you."

"Well, all I can say is thank God it's consigned to the history books," said Daniel.

A taxi arrived at 11.45 to take Diana and Garth back to the Raffles, and John and Tara made their way back next door after thanking Daniel and Linda for a thoroughly enjoyable evening.

CHAPTER 44

Daniel was in the office early the next morning to send some urgent emails off. Surprisingly, Luke arrived at 8.30. He put the kettle on, made his way to his desk, and started thumbing through the post, pausing to pick up the receiver as the phone rang.

"Yes he is, who may I say is calling? Sorry, who?" There was a pause. "Oh. Oh I see. Hold on, I'll put you through."

Daniel looked at Luke quizzically. "Who is it?"

Luke hesitated for a moment as if lost in thought. "It's British Customs and Excise."

"Yeah right, stop mucking about. Who is it really?"

"I'm serious, you'd better take it."

Daniel picked up the phone and pushed the button to put the call through.

"Daniel Cassidy speaking, how can I help?"

"Mr Cassidy, this is Gill Bordeman from Her Majesty's Customs and Excise in London, although I am speaking to you from Singapore at the moment. Can you tell me about your involvement with a Mr Han Atima?"

Daniel swallowed hard and looked across at Luke, who had stopped dead to listen to the conversation.

"Er, we were going to buy some boats from him. Why do you ask?"

"I have to advise you at this stage that he is being held awaiting trial at the Old Bailey in London. Perhaps you would be kind enough to elaborate on the boats you were going to purchase from him?"

"What sort of things do you need to know?"

"Well, for a start, what were they made of?"

"Fibreglass."

"I see. If it is OK with you, a colleague and I would like to come and take a statement."

"OK, where do you want to meet?"

"At your home, I would suggest, and as soon as possible. How about 4pm this afternoon?"

"Sure, that's fine. Do you want my address?"

"That's not necessary, we already have it."

"Oh, I see. This sounds pretty serious."

"We have apprehended Mr Atima with approximately thirty million pounds' worth of heroin. I would ask you not to attempt to leave the country until we have spoken with you."

"OK," Daniel feebly replaced the receiver.

At that moment Vera walked in with a beaming smile. It vanished when she saw Daniel, who was now white as a sheet.

"Are you all right?" she asked.

"Well, what was all that about?" Luke asked almost simultaneously.

"You're not going to believe this."

"Go on," said Luke.

"My intuition was right. Han has just been caught importing thirty million pounds' worth of heroin into the UK."

Vera's jaw dropped and her eyes widened in horror. "How did they catch him?"

"I don't know yet, but they're coming to see me this afternoon at home. He's apparently due for trial at the Old Bailey."

"And you're in the middle of it," Luke said. "What does this mean?"

"I don't know yet, I'll tell you when they let me know more later."

They sat in silence for a few moments before Daniel said, "Can you cope without me today? I think I'd better go home now."

"Yes, sure" said Luke. "I'll give you a bell later."

***

Linda was on the veranda with Sam when Daniel arrived home, and got up to see who it was. She went and opened the door, took one look at Daniel getting out of the car, and asked, "What's wrong?"

"Put the kettle on while I change, and I'll tell you— you're not going to believe this."

"Now I'm intrigued."

She disappeared into the kitchen as Daniel made his way upstairs. He got out of his work clothes and put on a pair of swimming shorts, then made his way back down to the veranda.

"So what's all this about?" she inquired.

"UK Customs apparently caught Han with thirty million pounds' worth of heroin hidden inside two boats."

"Oh my God!" Linda put her hand to her mouth, wide-eyed with shock. Sue Lee appeared at that moment to ask if they wanted drinks, as the kettle had just boiled.

"Er...yes please," answered Linda without taking her eyes off of Daniel.

Sensing the mood and seeing Sam's puzzled face, Sue Lee led the little boy away. Linda went to sit by Daniel.

"Well this is a turn up for the books!" she said. "I'm glad you had nothing whatsoever to do with them. In any case, how do you know all this?"

"They're coming to interview me this afternoon."

"Oh my God!"

***

By 4pm, they were ready and waiting for the customs officers, Daniel pacing between the sitting room and the hall and peering out at the drive every few minutes. Gill and Grant arrived along with a uniformed Singapore Police officer and a member of the Singapore Customs investigations unit. Sue

Lee showed them through to the veranda where Daniel and Linda were waiting. Introductions were made, and Linda politely asked if they needed anything.

"I'd appreciate a decent cup of tea with fresh milk," Grant smiled. "I've had nothing but UHT since I left England."

"We can certainly sort that out for you," Linda replied, instructing Sue Lee accordingly.

Once she had left, Gill launched straight into the reason for their call, and that they had found Daniel's telephone number and details in Han's diary.

"You mentioned on the phone that you were looking at importing some boats from him," she said. "Can you tell us how this came about, from the beginning?"

Daniel started with the sacking of Gordon Burrage, and explained that he had committed suicide shortly afterwards.

"OK, we'll make some inquiries with Surrey Police on that when we return," Gill said, making notes. "Tell us about Edward Lim."

As Daniel spoke, a torrent of further questions came forth. Where and how had they met, and what was his involvement as far as Daniel was concerned? Daniel mentioned the meeting with him in Istanbul, recounting the story of his whole experience there, but did not discuss his suspicions.

"Do you have any further information that we can link with him?" she asked.

"No, nothing at all other than what I have told you."

"I do remember his car," Linda, who had been silent until now, cut in. All eyes turned in her direction. "It was a white Mercedes."

"Can you be a bit more specific?" one of the Singapore officers asked.

"It was one of the big saloons, and it had black and white number plates."

"Malaysian registered, by the sounds of it," the officer muttered.

"It also had a big dent down one side. Now I think about it, I actually saw it sitting in a drive when I came home one day. He came round shortly after and I was sure I had seen it before." She turned to Daniel. "It was one of the ones you like, the one the Barratts drive."

"Ah, that would be the latest S Class if that's the case."

"Thank you Mrs Cassidy, that's most helpful. Is there anything else you can think of?"

"Not for the moment. To be honest, the news has really shaken both of us badly."

"I'm sure it has," said Gill.

One of the Singapore officers excused himself after asking if he could use the phone to reach one of his colleagues. He stood in the hall issuing instructions to send someone to the Tanglin Club to get everything they could from there, and sent a team up to the causeway to go through any film they had of vehicles of the Merc's description entering or leaving.

While he was gone, Grant picked up the investigation from the British perspective and asked more in-depth questions about Turkey.

"Do you know where the factory he took you to was?"

"No, I don't. He never mentioned the name of the place."

"That doesn't surprise me, somehow."

"We went into the Asian side of Istanbul, crossed a stretch of water on a ferry, and then drove for about two hours. We came off the main road and onto a dirt track. The name that kept appearing on the signs was Burtha or Burka or something."

"Borsa, perhaps?"

"Yes, that was it, Borsa. We turned off before the signs said we were in it."

"Excuse me a minute." Grant got up and pulled Gill aside to confer for a moment, then pulled out his mobile phone. He phoned the office and informed them of the approximate geographic location of the factory to relay directly to the authorities in Istanbul.

Once that was done, he sat back down.

"We are going to have to ask you to give evidence at the trial in London in the near future. Would you be happy to do so?"

"Well, I'm not sure. Would I be in danger?"

"As far as giving evidence is concerned, I'm not going to beat around the bush," said Grant. "If you choose not to give evidence voluntarily, you will be subpoenaed to do so. I hope that makes it clearer?"

Daniel was silent for a moment, and his face reddened.

"Can you assure me that my family and I are in no danger? You must appreciate the position I'm in!" he said irritably.

"We fully appreciate your situation, Mr Cassidy, but none of this is of our making," Gill responded. "While I would like to be able to say that you are in no danger, I'm afraid that I cannot give you that guarantee. The only thing we could arrange is to put you and your family in the witness protection programme."

"I have a business to run, and family and friends to consider. That's not even an option!"

"The choice is yours."

The true weight of what they were embroiled in was beginning to hit home. The more it did, the more Daniel realised he was between a rock and a hard place he could not get out of.

"In the meantime, we need a statement from you," Gill said, getting out an official-looking pad. "I need you to run through the whole story again I'm afraid. I'm sorry for both of you, but the sooner we get these people behind bars, the better."

"We understand you're only doing your job, but I wish we weren't involved," Daniel sighed.

"You've got Mr Lim and Han to thank for involving you, I'm afraid."

"Yes, I know. I should have listened to my instinct."

"What makes you say that?" asked Grant.

"Well, if I'm honest, the whole thing appeared fishy from the word go. There was something off about the way they wanted to conduct business, structure the deal, and so on, but I decided to ignore my gut feeling, thinking it was a good business proposition. How wrong I was!"

In the hall, the phone rang. It was Luke; Linda brought him up to date while Daniel gave Customs the statement they wanted.

As she hung up, a taxi arrived carrying Diana and Garth. Daniel and Linda had arranged to take them to Jumbo Seafood that night, but in the shock and confusion of the day, they had forgotten. Linda quickly showed them into the sitting room, where she poured them a gin and tonic and explained the day's events.

"I simply can't believe it!" Diana exclaimed. "I feel awful for having such a good laugh about it last night."

"Oh I shouldn't think twice about that. After all, some of the events seem pretty comical in retrospect."

"Well, I only hope the rest of the saga turns out the same way! Poor old Daniel."

"I certainly hope you're right."

In the next room, Grant asked Daniel when he was planning to visit the UK again, and advised him he would have to spend some time there during the trial, though they would give him notice as to when this was likely to be. Fifteen minutes later, they had wrapped everything up.

"If you remember anything else at all, please ring me, day or night," said Grant, producing two cards. "If anything suspicious happens or you're worried about anything at all, call either us or the Singapore police any time. The authorities here are fully aware of the situation and will support you should you need it. We'll see you back in the UK."

Daniel took the two cards, shook hands with them all and bid them goodbye, walking into the sitting room with a sigh.

"I think I need a drink."

"All in hand," Linda said as she produced an ice-cold gin and tonic from the bar fridge and handed it to him.

"Sounds like you've had a hell of a day," Garth said, shaking his head. "You probably don't feel like going out this evening. We can make ourselves scarce, if you like?"

"No. I won't hear of it, it won't do me any good to sit and brood. We'd be far better off going to dinner; It won't take me long to have a quick shower and change."

The conversation at dinner that evening was dominated by speculation and intrigue about what had been going on, as well as what the outcome would be. One thing was certain; HM Customs knew Daniel was innocent of any involvement. What was up for debate were the whereabouts of Edward Lim, and the part he played.

CHAPTER 45

Despite being meticulously careful for the most part, Xu's ambition and greed had made him overlook one aspect that threatened his anonymity; his car in Singapore.

Singapore Immigration had sifted through hours of video footage, and had been surprised to find that over the course of a month, hundreds of white Malaysian-registered Mercedes had made the crossing over the causeway. Fortunately, the vast majority were dismissed as being the wrong model or too old, which finally left them with 12 possible vehicles. They met with one of the police commissioners in Malaysia, who assured them he would get some answers.

It was suspected that Xu Xiang's car was not registered to him directly, but to a small office in Kuala Lumpur that was kept more or less as a mailbox. They had narrowed the field down to three vehicles. The police had spoken to the owners of two of them, but every time they had been to the office of the third owner, there had been nobody there. They placed it under observation to try to catch them for questioning.

Finally, the white Mercedes arrived with Xu at the wheel, on his standard post-collection run. They waited for him to enter the office, and then went up to knock on the door.

On seeing the police, Xu looked most uncomfortable, something that was noted by the officers. He told them his company owned the car.

They suggested that he had driven the car into Singapore recently. He denied this, but they pushed him further, requesting to look at his passport. Xu suddenly 'remembered' that he had visited Singapore to do some shopping, and had stayed with some friends for a few days. How silly of him to have forgotten! The police took down his personal details and had them authenticated before they left.

They felt sure that this was the man they were looking for, but would report back to the Singaporean and British authorities before taking it further. They needed to find some evidence linking him to the drugs.

Immediately after the police had left, Xu picked up the phone to one of his colleagues in Singapore. He would stop this from going any further right now. He knew that Daniel and Linda were the only ones who might identify him. Han would certainly keep quiet—he knew only too well the consequences of not doing so.

***

Grant was delighted to hear that they had a suspect, and suggested putting together an identity parade for Daniel and Linda. This would at least allow the man in question to be held while further investigations were made. The Singaporeans agreed, and the Malaysians said they could set it up the following week to be held in Kuala Lumpur.

Gill rang the Cassidy house to pass on that they would need to travel to Kuala Lumpur the following week. Linda said she would let Daniel know.

"While you are here," said Linda, "Daniel and I remembered that he took some photos of the boats being offered to him while he was at the factory in Turkey. We wondered if they would be of any help?"

"They most certainly would, I'll hop in a taxi now and come over."

***

Linda was the only one home that afternoon. Daniel was at work in Beach Road, and Sue Lee had taken Sam down to the local market. With his blond curls and endearing smile, Sam was becoming quite a celebrity during their morning trips to buy vegetables for dinner. Sue Lee was fitting in extremely well, and Daniel and Linda were delighted. They trusted her implicitly, and by insisting on doing much of the food shopping, she was saving both Linda's time and an enormous amount of money.

This particular afternoon, Sue Lee was quite oblivious to the fact that she was in fact being followed, and had been from the moment she had left home. The young Chinese man was dressed entirely in black, and surreptitiously followed her every move. He waited until Sue Lee had done her shopping and was on her own with Sam before he made his move.

He approached them from behind, and simply asked in a quiet even voice, speaking fluent Cantonese, "Are you the *amah* to the Cassidy family?"

Sue Lee turned round quickly; surprised that someone had managed to sneak up on her so quietly. She noted his cold, humourless eyes, and knew he was trouble.

***

Gill Bordeman arrived at about 3.30 that afternoon. Linda invited her through to the veranda, where they enjoyed a glass of Coca Cola before Linda went and fetched the photos.

Gill looked at the photographs carefully, inspecting each one at length.

Linda asked how the photos could be of any help; seeing that they had caught the perpetrators red-handed and had all the evidence they needed to convict them.

Gill apologised that she could not discuss things in any greater detail, but reassured Linda that it all went towards building the larger picture.

It was as they were sitting talking that Sue Lee arrived home with Sam, and walked through to where Gill and Linda were sitting.

"Sorry to disturb you, Mem, but man give me this for you."

"Oh, thank you Sue Lee," Linda said, slightly puzzled, as she took the envelope "Which man?"

"When we go out, Mem. The man come up to me when we finish shopping."

Linda looked at the envelope. It was addressed to 'Casity', in bold type on the front. Linda looked at Gill. "How very odd," she said as she opened the envelope.

Gill noticed Linda go pale as she read the note, which had been typed on lined A4 paper straight from a pad. The note simply said:

CASITY FAMILY

YOUR SON IS CUTE. HE WILL NOT BE IF YOU SAY OR DO ANYTHING TO HELP A CONVICTION. DO NOT MENTON THIS TO AUTHORITES OR YOU WILL REGRET. I HAVE PEOPLE WATCHING YOU. PLAY BY OUR RULES AND YOU WILL NOT SUFFER.

"What is it?" said Gill, noting Linda's distress.

Linda handed the sheet to Gill, then went over to Sue Lee. "Did the man touch Sam?"

"No Mem, just give the letter."

As Gill read the note, Linda picked up the cordless phone and called Daniel's office, where Vera put her straight through. At the sound of Daniel's voice, Linda broke down.

"Please come home," was all she could say.

Gill gently took the phone from Linda and explained to Daniel what had happened.

Daniel, in his frustration, rounded on her. "This is all your bloody fault! if you had left us alone none, of this would have happened. I'm on my way home, and I hope none of your bloody lot are there when I get there."

Gill understood, but did not bother to answer. She knew he would calm down on the drive home. Instead, she said a polite goodbye and rang Grant on her mobile to update him. He was disturbed by the news, to say the least.

"Shit! I'm glad you were there when it came to light, or we might never have known," he remarked. "It proves that we have touched a nerve somewhere. It could be from someone questioned in Malaysia, or perhaps Han's side of things, because the worry is of a conviction. I'll be there in 20 minutes."

He arrived at the Cassidy house in a police car along with the Singapore Customs officers in charge of the case at exactly the same time as Daniel.

Gill was right. Daniel had indeed thought about what he had said, and apologised.

"Where's Linda?" he asked.

"She has gone upstairs for a while," Gill responded.

Daniel dashed upstairs, where he found Linda sitting on the bed hugging Sam. Daniel sat next to them, and they drew strength from each other for several minutes as Linda sobbed quietly. They both knew how real the danger was.

Sue Lee showed Grant and the others through to the veranda, where they all examined the letter through latex gloves. They did not want to put any more prints on it before forensics had had their turn.

Daniel, Linda, and Sam came down after about fifteen minutes, and Daniel read the letter himself. Grant watched him carefully, gauging his reaction. He knew that the whole case hinged on Daniel's co-operation.

"We don't know who's behind the letter. It could have been written on the instruction of Han, or by the elusive Mr Lim," he said. "Either way, it's essential that we try to identify the person they're picking up for questioning in Malaysia."

"Grant, it really is irrelevant to us which one of them is behind it. It was delivered to my *amah* and son not half a kilometre from our house. Call me neurotic, but that leaves me feeling mighty vulnerable, because whoever it was, they're bloody well watching us!"

"Yes, that they may be, but the nature of the letter is a to prevent you from giving evidence against *someone*."

"Yes, and if I had my way I wouldn't give evidence, not under the circumstances."

"The police will keep you under observation until we can think of something. They'll have a car outside at all times, and you'll be escorted if you need to go out."

"Bloody marvellous, now we're under house arrest!"

"Not at all. It's simply a way of trying to secure your safety for the immediate future," Grant said forcefully.

"Daniel," Linda spoke for the first time. "Let's just go along with it until we can think about it more rationally."

Daniel sighed, "OK."

Grant and Gill promised to try and bring the trial in the UK forward under the circumstances, and departed with the letter once another car had arrived to keep watch. They knew that time was of the essence now, and that they needed to get the identity parade done before anything else stopped Daniel and Linda from giving evidence willingly. Singapore police had already asked the Malaysians to arrest the man known as Xu for further questioning, and hold him until the identity parade had taken place.

***

Xu received the phone call that afternoon, and was advised that the house had been swarming with police almost as soon as the letter had been delivered. Xu was seething with anger, and instructed the next move. He would stop this at all costs.

Xu's protégé in Singapore reacted quickly to his request, and at 1am the following morning was heading back towards the Cassidy house. He left his car on the main road, recovered a bag from the boot, put a rucksack on his back, and headed up the winding road into the park on foot. He rounded the bend and could see the house ahead of him, its porch and veranda lights on even though there was no movement. He headed around the side of the house to the back door that entered the kitchen.

He had not spotted the unmarked police car that was tucked away in the drive opposite, but the two officers inside had not seen him slip round the side of the house either. They had the radio on, and were busy smoking and chatting with no inkling that something was going on under their noses.

The man tried the shutter. It was, as expected, unlatched, though the security grilles behind it were firmly locked. He opened the shutter quietly and brought the bag up to the grille, spotting the moonlit outline of a dog sleeping against the far wall of the kitchen.

He opened the mouth of the bag carefully and held it against the grille, making sure his hands were nowhere near it. He balanced his rucksack on his knee and brought it up under the bag, lifting the contents until they fell against the grille.

The bag came to life as a large black cobra slithered to freedom and threaded its way into the kitchen.

Once the snake had moved, the man gathered the bag up and placed it in his rucksack before carefully closing the shutter and retracing his steps.

***

One of the officers in the car was in the middle of a story his colleague had heard many times before when he thought he saw something move near the side gate. He sat up and stared at the spot. His colleague followed the line of his gaze.

"There is someone by that gate, I'm sure of it."

"Probably just the movement of the branches in the breeze."

"No, there is someone coming out of the gate, Look, Look!"

"Ssh! Yes, you're right."

"Let him get past that next drive, and we'll get him when there is nowhere for him to run."

They watched him walk past the next drive. He scanned the road, eyes everywhere. The car leapt forward out of the drive, blue lights illuminated.

The man immediately broke into a run. He tried to clear a steep bank on one side of the road, and was nearly at the top when he lost his footing and fell heavily, ending up in one of the large storm drains.

The two officers piled out of the car and were on top of him in no time. They had not expected him to run, despite their earlier comment, but in doing so he had proved himself guilty of something.

Once they had him in cuffs and had searched his person, they radioed in to the station and gave them details from his ID card; he was a Mr Henry Ong.

"What were you doing coming out of the garden of that house, Henry?" the officer that held him pressed.

No response.

"What were you doing coming from that house?" he repeated.

Still no response.

The other officer searched through his rucksack while standing at the open boot of the car.

"There is absolutely nothing in here. Seems a bit odd to be carrying an empty rucksack, doesn't it, Henry?"

"I was just using their garden as a shortcut," he responded in a snarl.

The tone of his voice reassured them that they had caught him up to no good, and they summoned a second car from the station to come and take over while they took him in for further questioning.

"And just where were you heading that necessitated a short cut at one in the morning?"

No response.

They bundled him into the back of the car and went back up to the Cassidy house. One of them stayed with Henry while the other went around the house to see if there was any sign of a break-in or damage. There was none, and all the security grilles were still locked.

"All appears OK," he reported back.

They continued to try and question the suspect, but got nothing further from him. About 20 minutes passed before a second car arrived to relieve them from their surveillance duties, and they headed back to the station to question the obstinate Mr Ong further. They would keep him in until they had spoken to the Cassidy family the following morning to check all was OK, choosing not to wake them for now; they did not want to worry the family any more.

CHAPTER 46

Sue Lee was the first to enter the kitchen the next morning, opening the shutters and unlocking the grilles as normal. Skipper raised his head, took one look at Sue Lee, and then closed his eyes, deciding that sleep was still the best option.

Sue Lee wandered round the rest of the floor as usual and started her normal routine of sweeping. As she went back into the kitchen to get a mop, she saw a policeman in the doorway and jumped. He had come over to check that all was OK.

Sue Lee advised them that everything was fine, and he returned to the car. They radioed in to the station to let them know that all appeared normal, and that they would have to release Henry Ong.

Linda wandered down to the kitchen in her dressing gown to find a pot of tea ready and waiting for her to take back upstairs. This told Skipper that the day had begun, and he greeted Linda with loud whines and a wagging tail. Linda put the pot and a couple of mugs on a tray and made her way back to the bedroom, leaving Skipper looking dejected.

The noise Skipper had made greeting Linda had also awoken the other creature lurking in the kitchen. The cobra had headed for a dark corner of the kitchen and slithered into the gap between the refrigerator and the wall, where it had coiled up, invisible to all until now.

Sue Lee was walking back from her quarters, hotly pursued by Skipper, and had just entered the kitchen when she saw the snake stretching half way across the kitchen floor, its tail still behind the fridge. It was heading in her direction. She let out a scream, then turned and ran to the dining room. Skipper immediately put his hackles up and started barking at it.

The cobra, now fully visible, arched its body and flared its neck, lifting its head two feet off the ground. It stared at the dog, tasting the air menacingly. Skipper lunged forward, and the cobra released its poison, striking him right in the eyes. The dog recoiled and ran back out into the garden, giving deafening howls of pain.

Daniel and Linda had heard the scream from Sue Lee and were already making their way downstairs when they heard the noise from Skipper. They ran down with no idea what to expect.

Daniel came to a sudden stop as he approached the kitchen. He was faced with the sight of Sue Lee at the back door wielding the pole that normally supported the centre of the washing line and using it to beat a large cobra. She had obviously struck it a few blows already, as it was having difficulty moving. The next blow caught it on the head, and it collapsed to the floor. Sue Lee kept on whacking until it was almost severed in two.

The two police officers appeared behind Sue Lee and watched as she finished the snake off. Sue Lee saw Linda standing behind Daniel and shouted, "Mem, Skipper, please look!"

Linda darted out of the dining room to find Skipper lying on his stomach, desperately trying to wipe his eyes with his front paws and making spine-chilling noises of distress.

"Skipper! Skipper!" Linda said shakily through tears. Hearing her voice, the dog stopped and tried to look at her, but it was obvious that he could not see. His eyes had swollen to the size of golf balls. She stroked him and tried to calm him down, calling desperately for Daniel.

Sue Lee, seeing the situation, yelled, "Water, get water sir!"

Daniel duly obliged, and quickly switched the hose on. Linda directed the water over Skipper's eyes while Sue Lee held him firm. He continued to whine louder as he fought to free himself from Sue Lee's grip. They continued to do this for about ten minutes before Daniel noticed the two police watching them, feeling a flash of anger at their presence.

"Shove off back to your car!" he shouted, before adding in a quieter voice, "You two useless lumps of lard."

"Daniel, that's not necessary!" Linda responded sharply.

The two policemen disappeared back to the car. Such situations were not uncommon in the tropics, and Sue Lee seemed to have it under control. They did not report the incident, which seemed unconnected to their duties.

Linda left Daniel and Sue Lee hosing down Skipper's eyes and returned to the house to call the vet, who advised them to continue doing exactly what they were doing. She explained that the swelling should go down and Skipper's sight should return to normal, but they needed to be sure that he had not actually been bitten. Sue Lee assured them that Skipper had not been close enough for that, and they all began to relax a little. They discussed the incident between themselves, and assumed that the snake had entered through the kitchen door early that morning; it was not uncommon for them to find snakes in the garden.

Eventually Skipper started to calm down and they led him to the veranda, where he lay with his head on Linda's foot. Daniel cautiously disposed of the dead snake, using a garden spade to chuck it into the undergrowth over the fence before he went to join Linda.

"I really can't stand the thought of being chaperoned," he said. "It's going to drive me mad. If we're going to be shot, what the hell are a couple of goons like that going to do to stop it? Absolutely bugger all, that's what."

"I can't say they make me feel that much more secure." Linda agreed, "I did wonder about going to stay with the Van de Berghs in Hong Kong for a while. Nobody would find us there."

"I should think that so long as the authorities know where we are it wouldn't be a problem, but we shouldn't impose any danger on anyone else."

"I'll ring them, fill them in, and see if they have any ideas. I would think they'd be delighted to help."

"Don't forget we can't do anything until the identity parade is over with."

"I know. Can you phone whoever is in charge of this charade and tell them to call their so-called protection off?"

"I'll give Grant a ring before he leaves for London and talk through it with him."

***

The Kuala Lumpur police had been keeping track of Xu's movements since they had first visited him, realising that this was quite possibly the man the British and Singaporean authorities were so keen to catch. They had started to delve into the financial status and activities of each of his companies, and quickly found they were unearthing quite a can of worms.

A day after the phone call from Henry in Singapore, there was a knock on Xu's door. He was asked if he would come down to the police station for questioning, and told in no uncertain terms that if he did not come with them of his own accord, he would be arrested.

He had already written note number two to the 'Casity' family, posted that day by a friend of his from a mailbox in Kuantan. He was sure it would do the trick—it had to.

***

Daniel spoke to Grant that evening. They discussed the merits and drawbacks of police protection, as well as what might happen next. Daniel made it quite clear that the officers shadowing them were to be called off. He also let Grant know that they would probably go to Hong Kong until they were due to give evidence in London. Grant was told him he was leaving with Gill that evening to try and pull the trial forward, so the Singapore officers would be taking them up to Kuala Lumpur for the identity parade.

The following day, both Linda and Daniel felt a little easier about life, and began to look forward to spending some time in Hong Kong. Linda and Sam would fly out first, with Daniel to follow about two and a half weeks later. They would stay there for a couple of weeks before hopefully heading back to London for the trial, although Daniel had been told it could be up to three months away.

Daniel was flicking through the post at the breakfast table that morning, when an envelope made him stop in his tracks. It was addressed, like the last, to the 'Casity' family.

Linda saw Daniel freeze and looked over at the letter.

"Oh my God!" she gasped.

"Well, I guess we had better see what our life expectancy is," muttered Daniel. "Just looking at the envelope won't help." He slid his finger under the flap and opened it along the seam, looking at the postmark as he did so. "Kuantan."

"Then it's definitely Edward Lim who feels threatened."

Linda watched anxiously as Daniel pulled the paper from the envelope.

The note read:

THE SNAKE WAS NO MISTAKE—YOU TALKED TO THE AUTHORITIES. IF THE DOG IS DEAD, TOO BAD— YOU TALK AGAIN IT WILL BE YOUR SON. I CAN REACH YOU WHEREVER YOU TRY TO HIDE.

"Now I really do feel unsafe," said Linda. "We've got to get straight out of here until the trial is over. We're not only being watched, but they are getting into our house, even with police protection. Do you think we should tell them?"

"No, honey, I don't. They'll just repeat what we've heard before. Have you mentioned Hong Kong to anyone?"

"No, why?"

"The fewer people know where we are, the less likelihood of the wrong people finding out. We'd better advise the Van de Berghs of that as well. I think you and Sam ought to come with me today. I don't feel happy about leaving you here alone."

"We'll just get in the way. Can't you work from home?"

"Yes, I suppose that makes better sense. I'll call Luke and Vera and update them."

***

The following morning, the police car arrived to take them up to Kuala Lumpur. Sam tagged along; they did not want to leave him with Sue Lee in case someone came for him. In fact, he had not been out of their sight since the second letter. They had even moved his little bed into their bedroom.

They crossed the causeway, passed through Immigration without having to queue—which was something of a novelty—and were soon on the high-speed highway running from Johor Baru up to Kuala Lumpur. Daniel and Linda were visibly nervous as they approached the police station, despite being assured by the officers accompanying them that there was no danger, and that at no time would they come into contact with any of the suspects.

They were driven straight in through some security gates at the rear of the building.

The building itself was not that old, but was already showing signs of heavy wear and tear. They walked up two floors and were taken into a briefing room, where they were offered a coffee and left alone. They did not discuss the matter at hand in case they were being listened to.

About an hour later, the officers returned and asked Linda to join them first. Linda and Daniel had assumed that they would be asked to identify the person together, so it came as a surprise to be taken separately.

Linda was taken down a flight of stairs to the end of the building and shown into a room with a wall made of one-way glass. She sat down and waited for the people to be brought in to the next room, watching as each of them filed into the room. She hid her recognition of suspect number five well.

The police waited until they had all entered the room before asking Linda to walk along the length of the glass and look at each of the suspects carefully to see if she recognised any of them. Linda got to the end of the row and announced that she did not. She was taken back upstairs, but to a different room to the one in which Daniel waited. Sam was brought in to join her.

Once Linda was seated in the waiting room, Daniel was asked to do the same, and gave the same verdict to the officers at the end of the parade.

Neither of them spoke on the way home in the car. They both felt guilty, but knew it was the only option they had had in the circumstances.

They arrived back in Singapore hoping that this would be the end of the threats, but knowing they had a long way to go yet. They sat down that night with large gin and tonics after putting Sam to bed, but the drinks did little to lift their moods.

***

The Malaysian police were disappointed at the outcome of the ID parade, but would nevertheless be charging Xu with the counts of fraud and embezzlement they were uncovering. He was not free yet, but when he was advised that the charges against him were now of a financial nature, and would be dealt with in Malaysia, Xu knew his threats had worked.

Singapore authorities were continuing to make inquiries as to the nature of Mr Lim's activities there, and had visited the Tanglin Club armed with photographs, but while they had sparked vague recognition in some of the staff, none of them could give a definite ID. They had done the same for the offices in the Shaw Centre, but the result was the same. Singapore Customs phoned Grant and Gill in London and let them know the outcome of the identity parade and investigation.

They too were disappointed that the lead seemed to be going nowhere, but concentrated on getting Han and Eugene put away.

CHAPTER 47

Linda and Sam were due to fly out to Hong Kong in two days' time. The couple were delighted to be of assistance, and Linda was assured that they were welcome to stay for as long as they liked.

Keanu and Kate Van de Bergh were Americans who had lived in Hong Kong for about seven years. They had no children, but adored Sam, spoiling him rotten whenever they could. Keanu was in his late thirties; dark haired, fit, and good looking, sporting a permanent tan from the water skiing he did each weekend. He worked with an American bank, while Kate was a socially active housewife with natural blond hair and a superb figure.

The couple lived in Stanley on Hong Kong Island, owning a beautiful four-bedroomed house set high in the hills with its own pool and spectacular views of the bay below and the ocean beyond. A red Ferrari F360 Modena and a Silver Range Rover graced the drive. They were the envy of many.

They had first met Daniel and Linda while water skiing in Singapore many years before. From then on, they met up at least four or five times a year, usually while Keanu was in Singapore on a business trip. They always stayed with the

Cassidys, much preferring home life to that of hotels, so were eager to return the favour now.

***

Linda spent the next couple of days packing up all they were likely to need for the following few weeks, and was standing looking at the packed cases when Daniel walked in from work on the day before they were due to leave. As soon as she saw him, she started to sob uncontrollably. Although they had both decided there was very little risk now, she did not want to leave Daniel alone in the house. She was worried, angry, and upset that this turn of events had been forced upon them.

Daniel held her and stroked her head until she finally stopped.

"Look at the mess you've made of my shirt," he said light-heartedly.

Linda looked at the wet patch covered with mascara and lipstick and started to giggle.

"You know I can't come with you straight away," he said, reading her thoughts. "I can't leave Luke to do it all. The sales side would be a disaster; you know how undiplomatic he is! Besides, there's no danger now."

"I wish I could believe you, but Han is not going to go down quietly, is he?"

"I don't think he has a choice. It wasn't me who caught him with the drugs, there must have been other witnesses." He looked down at the luggage. "Bloody hell, I think we'd better charter a jet of our own if you're taking that lot!"

Linda looked at the luggage again, and the tears returned.

"It's only going to be a few weeks, we'll be at home in Sussex before long!" said Daniel. "I'm sure you don't need that much!"

This criticism pushed Linda her over the edge. "Right!" she said as she unlatched and picked up one of the cases. "You can pack the bloody things yourself!" The case fell open, and the contents fell all over the floor. Daniel watched in disbelief as Linda repeated this with each packed case, and turned to walk away.

"If I'm missing something when I get to Hong Kong, don't bother following me there!" she bellowed after him through the tears.

Daniel was almost in tears himself at the sight of Linda so distressed, but he decided he had better leave her to get it out of her system rather than try to sort it out now. She needed to blow off steam.

"Did you bloody well hear me? Don't bother coming!" came the shout from the bedroom. Daniel continued to the bottom of the stairs as things went quiet, and told himself she would soon get over it.

He poured himself a whisky and sat out on the veranda, staring out onto the golf course.

"Everything OK, sir?" came Sue Lee's voice from behind him.

Daniel turned, " Yes thank you Sue Lee, Mem is just a bit upset, she'll be OK later."

"You want me to make supper, sir?"

"Yes, please, and can you get Sam ready for bed for me?"

"OK, sir." She duly disappeared back in the direction of the kitchen.

Daniel crept back upstairs and peered through the bedroom door. Linda was curled up with her eyes closed, silent and exhausted. He closed the door quietly and returned downstairs to his whisky.

Sue Lee gave Sam a bath, and Daniel went up to read his son a story before returning downstairs to have supper. He ate alone, having decided to let Linda sleep.

**

The next morning, Linda nestled up to Daniel and whispered an apology. They held each other tightly for a long time.

Daniel got up shortly afterwards and started to repack the suitcases with half as many clothes. Linda and Sam said goodbye to Sue Lee, and they got into the car. They drove in near silence to the airport; neither of them wanted to talk about what might happen. They checked the luggage in and went to have a coffee, going over the merits of not disclosing the snake attack to the authorities and pretending not to recognise Edward Lim. They were convinced it had saved their lives, for the moment.

Linda was in tears as they said goodbye, but Daniel told her to be strong.

"Ring me as soon as you get there, I'll be in the office." Daniel said as he wiped tears from her eyes.

"OK honey, I miss you already."

As soon as Linda had gone through Immigration she turned and gave one last wave to Daniel, who was by now choking up himself. When she had disappeared from sight, he walked back towards the car in the knowledge that his family was safe.

**

Their flight landed at 1.20pm, touching down at the recently completed Hong Kong International Airport. Having collected their cases, Linda saw Kate immediately, waving wildly and making her way to the gap in the barrier through which Linda and Sam would exit.

They greeted each other fondly before making their way to the car park, loading the cases into the back of the Range Rover, and heading off on the hour and a half's journey to Stanley. Kate could not wait to hear the details of what had been happening, and listened intently as Linda spoke.

They finally arrived at the house, and the electric gates swung open. Kate took one of the cases and showed Linda to her room. A large bouquet of flowers lay on the middle of her bed with a card bearing the words, '*Dearest Linda, you're welcome for as long as you need us. All our love, Keanu and Kate xxxxx'*. The gesture brought a tear to Linda's eye, but she held herself together and gave Kate a hug.

In Sam's room, they had bought sheets and curtains covered with Pooh Bear pictures, which, to Kate's delight, Sam immediately recognised. A large Pooh Bear plush sat in the middle of his bed, and he could not conceal his delight as he hugged it.

After Linda had phoned Daniel to tell him she had arrived safely, the three of them went down to the beach. Kate continued to question Linda on the events that had driven her to seek refuge with them, but agreed with their decisions on the identity parade and the snake incident. She too was sure it had probably saved their lives. It was something that Linda had needed to hear from someone other than Daniel, and made her feel much better.

When they returned to the house that afternoon, Keanu was already home. He too was delighted to see Linda, and they all sat round the pool drinking champagne while the maid prepared dinner.

Linda went through the story for a second time. Keanu listened carefully, stopping her every now and again to ask probing questions about the situation. He too endorsed their line of action, and said he and Kate would have done exactly the same thing.

"Well that is quite a story," Keanu concluded when Linda was finished, "it seems unbelievable."

"It's the sort of thing you read about every now and again, but you never expect it to happen to you," Kate added.

"Poor old Daniel. How's he coping with the pressure?" asked Keanu.

"Oh, you know what he's like, nothing really seems to faze him, but I think this is taking its toll. He's really trying to forget it until the trial."

"Not an easy thing, to be mixed up in something like this and try to forget it."

"Particularly as Customs have told him he's their number one witness."

"I only hope that the guy in prison doesn't know that."

"Well this is part of the worry. We may be out of the woods as far as Mr Lim is concerned, but what's the one who's about to get life in jail going to try?"

"I wouldn't think that they'll try anything in the UK," Kate reassured her. "They know that the authorities will be watching Daniel like a hawk."

"I hope you're right."

"I'm sure I'm right, but you'll be fine here for as long as you like, you know that."

"I really don't know what we would do without you."

Linda then excused herself to go and put Sam to bed. Kate insisted on reading him his bedtime story, much to his delight.

Over dinner, Keanu was on good form, telling stories and cracking jokes. As Linda laughed, Kate could see her stress melt away, and wondered how long it was since she had actually felt relaxed.

***

Daniel had driven straight from the airport to the office that morning, but was pleased to hear Linda's voice when she phoned, and even more cheered by how happy she had sounded.

That evening, he and Luke went to the Tanglin Club for dinner, during which he updated Luke on all the latest developments. Luke thought they had made the right decision, but warned that the worst was possibly still to come in the UK. Daniel pointed out that if Lim had been the mastermind, Han was possibly just a puppet without real contacts.

"In any case," he added, "we won't go back until just before the trial, and after it, whatever the result, the danger is gone."

"If you're not the one to put him away," Luke mused.

"Yes, I've been thinking about that. I'm going to answer the questions directly, without any elaboration or insinuation."

"I think that's all you can do. If you ask me, this guy deserves to go down for life anyway."

"Yes, he does, and I'm sure he will. They caught the guy red-handed, and they must have got their intelligence from somewhere, so why do they really need me?"

After a couple of bottles of red wine, they left the club in a taxi, planning to return for their cars the next morning.

In the taxi, Luke asked if he could stay at Daniel's that night, as he was not on the best of terms with Michelle. Daniel had been only too happy to oblige. Although he didn't admit it, he was relieved at the thought of having someone else in the house.

Daniel did not sleep particularly well for the next few nights, but as time went on and no more notes were forthcoming, he relaxed a little and began to sleep better. Luke stayed for three nights before venturing back home, only to return again the following night having had a blazing row.

***

The next few weeks seemed to fly past. Grant was in touch with Daniel twice a week, keeping him informed of likely trial dates, which were later and later each time they spoke. Daniel had a feeling that, in reality, he was just keeping tabs on his key witness.

Linda spoke to Daniel daily, and seemed extremely happy in her new surroundings, although she missed him desperately. He had delayed his trip to Hong Kong due the uncertainty of the trial date, which would have meant being away from the office indefinitely if he had left as planned. Linda had not been happy, but understood.

Five weeks after Linda had departed for Hong Kong, Daniel followed. The trial date had been confirmed; Daniel would spend a week with the Van de Berghs before he, Linda, and Sam went back to the UK, arriving a week before the trial.

Daniel touched down in Hong Kong to a rapturous welcome from everyone. When they arrived at the house, Kate took charge of Sam while Linda and Daniel disappeared upstairs to unpack and have a little time to themselves. It seemed as if they had been apart forever.

That evening, they gathered outside for drinks by the pool, followed by a superb roast turkey Kate had prepared specially for the occasion. After dinner, as Kate and Linda sat and chatted, Daniel and Keanu stood out on the pool veranda, looking out at the sea.

"So how are you really feeling at the moment? No pretence." Keanu asked.

Daniel swirled his glass of whisky as he thought about the answer. He really wasn't sure.

"I think I'm OK, but it really is a case of up one minute and down the next. I'm all right until I think about the trial, and what could be in store for me. To be honest, the whole thought of being at the Old Bailey fills me with dread. I've only ever seen it on the television, but the thought of being there as a key witness for the second largest drugs heist in UK history terrifies me. I've never run from anything in my life, but if I could run right now, I think I'd do the minute mile! I feel as if I've had enough stress to last me my entire lifetime."

"Well, why don't you stay here until the day before the trial? At least that way you know you're safe."

"That's kind, but I've been in touch with some friends who have a boat on the marina in Chichester. They've kindly offered it to us, and I may take them up on it; make it a bit of a holiday and tour the Solent for a week. It'll keep the mind occupied anyway."

"It sounds like a good idea to me. Does Linda know yet?"

"No, I only spoke to them a couple of days ago. I'll see how Linda feels about it when we get back. She loves the house over there and may just want to stay at home, we'll see."

They stood and chatted for a while longer before joining the ladies and retiring to bed. The next day, they all went to the beach, where Daniel and Keanu spent most of the time taking it in turns water skiing from Keanu and Kate's speedboat. It was the first day of pure leisure that they had had in a long time.

That evening, Keanu and Kate decided they were going to take Daniel and Linda to Lamma Island for seafood. The maid would babysit Sam. They got a taxi to Aberdeen, jumped on a sampan, and after a couple of minutes of negotiating between Keanu and the lady at the helm, were on their way out of the harbour and across to the island. The sea was slightly choppier than was ideal, and they arrived without incident, but Linda looked remarkably relieved to get off the sampan.

Lamma Island was an unusual place, with only a couple of thousand inhabitants and no cars at all. They walked up the concrete jetty, remarking on how quaint the bay looked with the lights of the restaurants and bars lining its shore and the backdrop of the hillside behind.

"This looks like stress-free living to me," Daniel remarked. Linda squeezed his hand, as if in agreement.

"It's a great place if you don't have an office on the other side of town to get to!" said Keanu.

"I think I would be lost if I had to rely on ferries and taxis every time I needed to go anywhere—I just couldn't imagine life without my car," Kate added.

"I'm sure you're right," said Daniel. "It's just that we feel like being recluses at the moment, so this seems like a dream."

After a superb meal of prawns, crayfish, and other seafood, they caught the last ferry of the day back to central Hong Kong, and took a taxi back to Stanley. Linda and Daniel felt more relaxed than they had for a long time.

The rest of the week seemed to go in much the same vein, and did them both good. The Van de Berghs offered Linda the option to stay, but she insisted on going back to

London as moral support for Daniel. They were due to leave on the Virgin Atlantic flight to Heathrow at 10.40 that evening, but that left the whole day to enjoy the beach and some more skiing.

***

The journey to the airport in the Range Rover that night was quiet in contrast to when they had collected Daniel. Keanu and Kate offered to take some leave and come to the UK to support them during the coming weeks. Daniel and Linda thanked them, but suggested that they visit them in Singapore later in the year instead, so they could all truly enjoy themselves.

The flight took off on schedule, and as soon as the 'FASTEN SEAT BELT' signs had gone off, Sam was fast asleep. Linda and Daniel waited until the meal had been served before they too settled down.

CHAPTER 48

Han was determined not to spend the rest of his life in jail, which under the current circumstances was almost a certainty. He had been caught red-handed by HM Customs, the proof was undeniable, and it was a major haul. He was rightly a very worried man.

His barrister had advised him of the gravity of the situation, and set out his best line of defence. He knew Han was likely to be in prison for the long run, but he would try every trick in the book first.

Maya had been staying in London in the weeks following Han's arrest, along with his mother. Han had given her a couple of phone numbers for friends in Istanbul and asked her to get them to come to London as soon as possible, saying he was going to need their help. Maya had not heard of these friends before, and was suitably suspicious. She had been playing the loyal wife, but doubted his innocence. If he was indeed proven guilty, this would be the last she would have to do with him. As a nurse, she had seen first-hand the damage that drugs could do, and could not believe the level to which he had apparently lowered himself.

Han on the other hand, had fallen out of love with Maya a long time ago, if indeed he had ever truly loved her. However, he knew that his best plan was to play the loyal, loving family man. Maya had been correct that he needed her, but not for the reasons she would have liked.

Unsurprisingly, he had not heard a word from Lim, and did not expect to now. Lim was going to be seriously angry that the deal had gone wrong, although Han was at a loss to know where, and was unsure how to explain it if he did get out. He was acutely aware of how disposable he was.

Han was determined that he could use Eugene to take the heat off of himself, but his barrister was not convinced. He had wondered whether Customs knew about Daniel, or whether they had told him of his fate yet, but that was soon answered when it was announced that Daniel Cassidy was to be one of the witnesses for the prosecution. Han, for a moment, felt humbled, and wondered what Daniel had thought when he found out the truth, as well as what Daniel could say to harm his defence. He had to think of everything Daniel knew, and either let his barrister know so that the best possible defence could be prepared, or ensure that Daniel did not say anything out of turn. He would talk to his two colleagues when they arrived from Turkey.

***

The flight touched down half an hour early, and after retrieving their luggage, Daniel, Linda and Sam made their way straight to the car rental desk. They were too drained to catch the bus to Gatwick, and needed to rent a car anyway; the BMW needed to be taxed and undergo an MOT before it was road legal again. They decided to return to the house for a few days before collecting their friends' boat in Chichester, which they had decided was a good idea, both for security and to keep their minds occupied.

As they waited at the desk, Daniel's mobile rang.

"Hi, Daniel, it's Grant. Welcome back to the UK."

"Thanks. How is it all stacking up?"

"Very well. We've built a fairly cast-iron case against both Han and his colleague, Eugene, and you'll be pleased to hear it's all going ahead on schedule."

"Oh yeah, I'm ecstatic," Daniel responded sarcastically.

Grant ignored the sentiment and carried on. "We have to meet. Where are you staying? At your place in Sussex?"

"Well that's where we are heading right now, yes, but we won't be there all the time. We have other plans for the week."

"I'll meet you down at the house this afternoon. There are several things I need to run through with you to finalise our case. I'll see you at what, four o'clock?"

"Oh. Yes, I suppose so," Daniel replied hesitantly.

"What was that all about?" Linda asked when he had hung up, realising they were back in the thick of it again already. Daniel told her about the meeting planned for that afternoon as they made their way to the rented VW Golf.

It took them 25 minutes to get the car, during which time Daniel commented a number of times that it would have been quicker on the bus. He was tired, irritable, and all too aware of the seriousness of his predicament. He had managed for the past few weeks by telling himself that the worry he faced was a thing of the future, a problem on a different continent. Unfortunately, it was a reality that Grant's phone call had jolted them back to.

It took them just over two hours to navigate five of the junctions on the M25 that morning. To make matters worse, Sam was now wide awake, and almost as if he sensed the unease of his parents, was unhappy, fidgety, and tearful, only causing more stress. Eventually, they finally left the motorway, and the atmosphere became a little more relaxed as Sam finally fell asleep. They arrived at the house about three and a half hours later, having stopped briefly to pick up a few essentials.

Linda was the first inside, and froze the moment she stepped through the door. Her sixth sense told her that something was amiss. The house was cold, but it was more than just that. Cautiously, she picked her way inside.

***

Han's friends paid him several visits in prison. They had all decided that Daniel was a threat, but worried that circumstance would put Han away even before he had the opportunity to say anything. Regardless, they needed to let Daniel know he was under observation, and that a further incriminating word would be unwise. The two free men had eventually located the Cassidy home, and after a couple of days of general observation, decided that it was uninhabited. It appeared that nobody had been there for quite a while, which they reported back to Han.

***

Daniel and Linda had only to move from the hall to the sitting room to have their worst suspicions confirmed. The room was in disarray, with drawers turned out, debris everywhere, and the window to the side of the sliding doors into the garden broken. Daniel phoned Grant immediately and told him that they had been broken into, although he and Linda had already convinced themselves it was a warning sign. Grant told Daniel to phone the police straight away, and said he would leave immediately to join them. He advised Daniel not to touch or move anything, but made no attempt to hide his worry about the situation.

It was too much for Linda. She had already been tired after the long flight, and simply sat on the sofa and burst into tears. After comforting her, Daniel's next call was to a glazier, as the wind and rain were blowing straight through the open hole in the window glass. Judging by the amount of water on the carpet, it had been doing so for some time.

As armed police began to arrive at the house and examine the chaos in the sitting room, Linda and Daniel went upstairs, hardly daring to look around them for fear of what they may find. All the drawers in their bedroom had been pulled from their runners and lay on the floor, their contents strewn across the carpet. They sat on their bed, and Linda fought fresh tears as she looked around her.

"Do you think this is a message that they can get to us?" she asked, looking earnestly at Daniel.

"It's either that or a hell of a cruel coincidence," Daniel replied. "On the face of it, there doesn't seem to be anything missing, so it can't have been a burglar. "

"Most of our valuable stuff is in Singapore," Linda pointed out.

"Yeah, but even the video recorder is still here."

Linda let a small smile come to her face. "That's probably because it's a vintage model."

"You're probably right, but if nothing is missing, the house was either disturbed for some other reason, or our friends have paid us a visit. I don't like it either way."

"Let's see what Grant makes of it."

They decided that they would tidy up, secure the house, and see what was missing, then go straight down to Tom and Mary's boat in Chichester as soon as Grant had left. Daniel phoned to explain that they might need to go to the boat that evening. Tom was horrified to hear about the break-in, and told Daniel that the boat was ready as soon as they wanted it. He said he would phone the harbour office, where he left a spare set of keys in case of an emergency, and ensure they would be available to Daniel at any time.

Shortly after Daniel spoke to Tom, Grant and Gill arrived on the scene. They introduced themselves to the officer in charge, who was sitting in the open tailgate of a Volvo T5 outside, getting their bearings before heading into the house.

Hearing the commotion outside, Daniel and Linda made their way downstairs to meet Grant and Gill in the hallway, and they all headed for the sitting room. The policeman who had been fingerprinting the room advised Linda that he had finished, so if she wanted to start clearing up, she could do so.

The four of them sat down, and a kind-faced officer asked if he could help by making them all a hot drink.

"Yes, thank you, that would be very kind. The milk is still on the floor of the Golf, and you'll find tea bags in the right hand unit above the hob," Linda advised him.

As soon as he had left, Gill got straight to the point. "I'm so sorry for what has happened here, it must have been an awful shock."

"You could put it that way," Daniel muttered drily.

"Anyhow," Gill continued, ignoring his comment, "we've spoken to the officer in charge. The team have picked up a lot of prints, but until they finish their sweep and take yours, we won't know if any were from the culprits. In a nutshell, we don't yet know whether this break-in is related to the trial or not, though the fact that there appears to be nothing missing is suspicious."

"We are going to have to keep an eye on you until the trial next week." Grant cut in, "I know you won't like it, but we cannot take any chances in light of what's happened."

Daniel put a hand on Linda's knee. "Don't worry about us. We won't feel comfortable here, so we've arranged to stay on a friend's boat on the Solent until the trial. We'll have the mobile."

Grant and Gill would have been happier finding Linda and Daniel a safe place of their choosing, but in the end they conceded that they were probably just as safe moving around, on the condition that they checked in every morning and evening to let Grant and Gill know where they were.

Daniel and Linda took a brief break to give their fingerprints for elimination and instruct the glazier, before Grant continued with some further questions that would hopefully help their case. While doing so, he touched on what had happened with the identity parade. Daniel and Linda said very little. Gill gave them a disappointed look with each vague answer, but they didn't care; at least they were alive.

Grant was soon on the phone arranging for an unmarked car to tail Linda and Daniel down to Chichester and ensure no one else was following them. As he did, Daniel retrieved Sam and called the UK office to explain the situation, and Linda went upstairs to gather some bedding.

Everything else would already be on the boat, they could buy food down there, and their suitcases were still in the car from the airport.

***

It was 6.30 that evening by the time they had they finally locked the house up and started on the 45-minute journey down to the marina. It had not been the afternoon of rest they had expected, and Daniel had to admit that he was on the verge of being too tired to drive.

It was on the A27 near Worthing that Daniel first noticed the red Vectra following them. He hoped it was Grant's tail and not someone else, but could not be too careful. He turned to Linda.

"Can you just ring Grant on the mobile, honey, and check that it's a red Vectra they have following us?"

Linda glanced at the mirror and dialled the number. "Hi, Grant, it's Linda Cassidy. Just quickly, can you confirm what type of car is supposed to be following us please? Is it a red Vectra?"

"I'll find out and ring you right back."

"He's finding out and ringing us back," Linda repeated to Daniel as she put the phone back in the door pocket.

"How on earth can he not know?"

"I suppose the car comes from the police and not from Customs, so he can't be expected to know them all."

"I guess you're right."

"Do you think we're being paranoid, honey?"

"Quite possibly, but I reckon we've a right to be after what has happened to us over the past few weeks."

Fortunately, Grant rang back within two or three minutes.

"Don't panic, it's ours, but you did the right thing to ring. If you have any suspicions about anything, you must let us know."

"OK, thank you. We'll see you next week, all being well."

"Don't worry, you'll see us all right. Have a good time."

CHAPTER 49

They continued their journey to the marina, arriving first at the harbour office to collect the keys, then at the other side of the marina to find the *Lady B*. They located the correct pontoon, parked the car as close to it as possible, and put Sam into his pushchair, having decided to open up before unloading their cases. Tom had told them she was moored against the end of the pontoon, and they walked there slowly, looking with interest at the various types of craft moored on either side on the way. As they reached the end of the marina, they looked up, and straight ahead of them was the *Lady B*. She was a Trader 41+2, only a couple of years old, and Mary and Tom had kept her immaculately. They climbed aboard, entering a teak-lined main saloon. Daniel turned on the power and they had a quick look round before going back to the car to collect the cases and the bedding. They spent the next hour organising themselves, feeding Sam and putting him to bed in the forward cabin.

Linda went to make their bed up and have a shower while Daniel left to collect their dinner from the chip shop in East Wittering. As he drove out of the marina, he spotted the Vectra sitting on the side of the perimeter road that gave its occupants a clear view of the *Lady B*. He found it faintly comforting to know someone was close at hand, although part of him was annoyed that such an invasion of his privacy and freedom was necessary. He longed for the following week, when it would all be over.

***

The following morning, they awoke to the creaking of their mooring warps, the clatter of the halyard on the neighbouring yacht, and the faint *slap-slap* of the wind-whipped waves against the hull.

"Sounds like the wind has gained strength overnight," Daniel muttered to Linda as he got up to make them both a cup of tea.

"Should be fun," Linda said with a smile as she glanced out of the porthole. Seeing the dark clouds, she pulled the duvet further up until it was round her neck.

As they sipped their tea, they decided that if the weather permitted, they would head out to Cowes on the Isle of Wight and spend a couple of days there. Once the plan was settled, they had a full English breakfast, and Daniel phoned Luke while it was still an acceptable hour in Singapore. He sorted out a couple of urgent business problems with the UK office, and when he was unable to stall any longer, he phoned his mother and brought her up to date with the latest situation, carefully playing down the potential danger they might be in.

With duty done, they wandered over to the marina shop to buy some provisions. The weather had turned out not to be too bad, but as they did not need to be anywhere in particular, they decided to wait until the following day before setting sail. It had stopped raining, but was damp, and the wind coming in off the coast was bracing. They were halfway back to the boat when Daniel's mobile rang. He picked it from his pocket, noticing that there was no caller ID.

"Hi, it's Daniel—" He stopped in his tracks, glanced at Linda, and then looked furtively around him.

Linda sensed something was wrong and stood motionless, staring into Daniel's eyes for a clue.

***

When they reported back, Han had been uptight about the fact that his friends had been unable to locate the Cassidys, who were obviously not staying at their house in the UK. Maybe they were still in Singapore?

He would have to get them to phone Daniel on his mobile. Although Customs had seized his Filofax with all his numbers in it, he knew he had the number on Daniel's card at home. He would get Maya to get hold of it.

The next time Maya visited him, Han asked her to get her mother to pass on Daniel's mobile phone number from the Istanbul house.

"Why do you want the number?" Maya had asked him warily.

"I want you to give it to the two friends who have come over."

"What for?"

"None of your business, just do as I say," Han replied sharply.

Maya picked up her handbag and left without replying. She had nothing further to say to him, but knew she had to do as she had been asked. She made the call to her mother in Istanbul, who was looking after the children for her. Maya had an uncomfortable feeling about what Han was planning, but if her fears were correct, she would make sure those plans were thwarted. She could have simply refused to get the number, but knew she had to do it so that Han would know nothing about it; she was quite sure of the consequences if he thought she was behind anything.

The next call Maya made was to David Armstrong, the barrister defending Han.

"Please don't let on that I have contacted you, but there is something you should be aware of," she said, before repeating what she had been asked to do.

"OK. Thank you Mrs Atima, I think I get the picture," he replied. "Leave it with me; I'll talk to your husband and advise him that Daniel Cassidy is no threat to him. Don't worry, I'll be diplomatic and he won't know we have spoken. If he's intending on threatening people, it will get him banged up permanently as quick as a flash."

***

After hanging up the phone, Armstrong immediately went across town to the prison where Han was being held. He had to convey his concerns to Han as subtly as possible before he did something stupid. David was shown in, and was seated in a meeting room when Han arrived. He wasted no time in getting straight to the point.

"As you know, our whole case is going to be an uphill struggle; you're telling me there was a money man who controlled you that you won't identify, but there's information both sides have access to suggesting that you had a partner. Quite frankly, the prosecution are going to rip you to shreds, and there's a good chance they'll prove that you did it willingly, and were in it from the start out of sheer greed."

There was a pause while an officer brought in cups of tea for them both. As soon as he had left, David resumed, "Daniel Cassidy is one of the key witnesses for the prosecution, and has mentioned a partner he was dealing with in his evidence. I think we can use him to your advantage. Because he has met your partner, he could help in your case, although he won't know it, and neither will the prosecution until he's on the stand."

Han looked at David quizzically. "What do you mean? How?"

"Believe me, he could be your biggest ally. It's good news that he will be testifying; there is very little he can say or do that is detrimental to your argument."

"But he is going to testify against me!"

"I know. You'll have to leave this one with me; I'll run through the final plans for the trial with you nearer the time, probably at the end of the week, but he's probably the only person that can save you from rotting in jail for the rest of your life."

David left Han looking a little bemused, but was fairly sure that he had understood. He only hoped that making it clear that they needed Daniel would save any threats. David knew that Customs were monitoring Daniel's every move and phone call. Surely Han would not be so naïve as to try and interfere with a witness?

***

David called Maya back to let her know that he thought he had got the message across, but did not elaborate on any of the detail. She just hoped he was right.

When she went in to visit Han the next morning, the first thing he asked was whether or not Maya had given the phone number to his friends.

"Not yet, I have only just had the call back from my mother."

"Get out of here now, go and phone it through to them straight away!" he shouted.

Maya knew that David's message had probably fallen on deaf ears, but then Han always did think he knew better than anyone else. She left the prison and wandered back to the hotel. She was in no hurry to give them the number, but knew that she had to.

About an hour later, one of the associates' mobiles rang, and Maya reeled off the number on the other end. They wasted no time in finding a public phone box and making their call.

***

"Mr Daniel, you don't know me, but I know you and your family very well. You are a witness at my friend's trial next week. Be careful about what you say. We know where you are. We are watching you all the time."

The line went dead.

Daniel repeated the message word for word to Linda, and they both looked around them. They were not far from where the Vectra had been parked the previous night, so they walked briskly in that direction. As they did, Daniel's mobile rang again. It was Grant.

"Daniel, don't worry about the call you just received, they're bluffing."

"How do you know about the call? And how do you know they are bluffing?"

"All calls to your mobile are being monitored. We're sure nobody knows where you are; we've had people on the marina gates all night. It's just a bluff to frighten you into perjuring yourself in court. I cannot stress enough, don't listen to it."

Daniel was furious at the invasion of his privacy. He switched his phone off and shoved it back into his pocket, then held a hand out to Linda.

"Come on honey, we'll go out today. Stuff the wind, we need a change of scenery," he said.

As soon as they were on board, he double-checked the tide times to ensure they would be able to get the *Lady B* through the channel on the other side of the lock. They were fine for another hour.

Without wasting any further time, Daniel put the keys in and fired up the port engine, waiting for it to settle into a steady idle before he fired up the starboard engine. He would let them both warm up for five minutes before slipping the mooring.

"We're going to have to lock out, honey. Can you put some more fenders down the starboard side?" he called to Linda?

"OK."

He went on deck, released the spring line, and neatly coiled it into a locker on the aft deck. The wind was pushing them on to the pontoon, so after a few more minutes of warming the engines, he let the bow line go and asked Linda to hold the stern line and jump on when he asked her to do so. They left the pontoon without incident, as if they did it every day.

As they approached the lock, Daniel looked at the boats surrounding them and then at the lock again. He had to admit he was worried; the lock looked as if it would only just take the boat. He carefully and slowly coaxed her in. It took every ounce of his concentration, but she finally fell into place. The lock keeper threw the bow line down to Linda, who was waiting on the deck. Daniel darted to the back of the boat to catch the stern line. The water was released from the lock gates and the boat tugged at her restraining lines as the water level dropped. Finally, the gates opened fully.

As Daniel was going back to the helm, he noticed a couple of men standing at the railings of the lock watching them. The lock keeper asked in a cheery manner where they were going, but both Linda and Daniel ignored him, assuming he would think that they had not heard. Within seconds, the Lady B was roaring out of the lock.

Daniel looked back to see one of the two men who had been watching them in the lock talking into a mobile phone. He knew then that they were Grant's men, and wondered where they would catch up with him.

Paranoid about his lack of privacy, Daniel wanted to get out of the area as soon as he could. He nudged the throttles forward, knowing he was already exceeding the speed limit through the moorings at Itchenor. About forty minutes later they reached the Chichester Bar beacon and open water. He opened the throttles to the stops. The *Lady B* gradually increased her speed, and they settled on their course through the old wartime forts, past Portsmouth, and onward to Cowes.

Linda had been with Sam down in the saloon during the first hour, but she was finding it a little difficult below now they were underway, so they both joined Daniel on the helm seat. They enjoyed the passing scenery together, waiting for smoother waters.

"I wish we could just go to France and forget the whole thing, as if it was a nightmare," Linda suggested.

Daniel was quick to reply. "Don't tempt me, honey. If only!"

***

They arrived in Cowes late that afternoon and were directed to a visitors' mooring, where they made sure the *Lady B* was secure before sorting themselves out. As they sat in the saloon taking in their surroundings, Daniel saw two men standing at the railings, looking in their direction. It was the same two who had been in Chichester.

"That didn't take long. In fact, I'd say Grant's boys were here before us."

"Why doesn't that surprise me?" Linda asked sarcastically.

"I thought they'd track us too. Anyway, only another few days to endure."

***

Han was getting more and more frustrated by the day. His friends were getting nowhere in their efforts to locate Daniel, even though they had long dispensed with the idea of being discreet. He wanted them to be seen, to emphasise that he could reach the Cassidys despite being locked up. The two men had staked out the Cassidy home, but had seen no movement in or out. They couldn't even phone to threaten him, as his mobile was apparently off.

He was more pissed off by the fact that they couldn't find the family than anything else. Some of what his barrister had said had sunk in, but he still wanted them to know that he was in charge. He told his friends to keep looking.

***

Robin, one of the two plain-clothed police officers tailing Daniel and Linda, walked down the pontoon. He had seen the *Lady B* come in to the marina, but waited for Daniel and Linda to settle in before disturbing them. Daniel saw him coming, but waited for him to knock on the hull of the boat before going out on deck to talk to him.

Robin introduced himself, and they shook hands.

"Mr Cassidy, I have a formal request from my boss asking if you could please contact Grant at Customs as he needs to talk with you urgently."

"Does he indeed? OK, thank you, I'll give him a buzz."
Daniel turned to go back into the boat, but Robin hung back

"Er, Mr Cassidy—it is urgent, sir."

"It always is, Robin," Daniel sighed. "Don't worry, I'll ring him now."

Daniel went back aboard, grabbed his mobile from the dashboard, and switched it back on.

"What did he want?" Linda asked.

"Grant wants me, apparently."

Daniel dialled out, and Grant picked up on the first ring. "Grant, it's Daniel, I gather from our accompanying convoy that you wanted to talk to me?"

"Yes, thanks for ringing. The police are continuing with their investigations into your break-in, and they have come up with several other prints. If we're going to prove whether or not it was you-know-who's merry band of men we're going to need to fingerprint any guests you may have had staying with you recently to eliminate them."

"Luke and Michelle are the only guests we've had. They are due over here next week, so you can ask them then."

"That's your partner in Singapore, I assume?"

"Yes, him and his other half."

"OK. By the way, I understand you're in Cowes at the moment. Please keep us abreast of your movements, it's so much easier than having to work it out."

"All being well, we will probably stay here until the day before the trial, when we'll head back to Chichester. Linda's not a great lover of the sea."

"OK. If you talk to Luke before he arrives, can you let him know what we need?"

"Yes, will do."

"We'll see you Monday at ten sharp. You're happy that you know where to go?"

"I'm not happy, exactly, but yes, I know where to go, I've had a look at an A to Z."

"Excellent! Don't worry, it'll all be over by next week. See you then."

That evening, Daniel and Linda wandered up through the steeply sloping street of the town centre along with Sam in his pushchair. They stopped at a little pizzeria for a spot of supper. As they entered, they had passed Robin and his colleague, and exchanged hellos.

Sam was beginning to get irritable toward the end of the meal, so they left to make their way back to the boat. They bathed Sam and put him to bed before retiring on to the aft deck, where they sat in the evening sun. The wind had abated, and they had a couple of drinks, which helped to relax Daniel enough to be able to chat at length to a doctor and his wife on the yacht moored next to them. They eventually parted ways, and Daniel and Linda watched the evening news before showering and going to bed.

***

Linda felt the slight jolt against the *Lady B*'s hull first. She opened her eyes, and sat half upright in bed. There was no further noise for a few seconds, so she put her head back down. Just as she did so she heard the thud of someone on the deck above her. She nearly screamed in fright, but managed to catch herself, and instead leaned over and rocked Daniel hard.

"There's someone trying to get in."

"What, what are you on about?"

"There is someone trying to get into the boat."

"You sure?" Daniel said. He sat up, all his senses suddenly on maximum.

"Yes, listen."

Within a few moments, Daniel too heard movement up above. He threw the duvet off, and was on his feet in milliseconds. He got his bathrobe off the back of the door and quietly made his way to the galley, where he picked up a kitchen knife. He continued quietly, listening hard. By the dim gloom of the lights on the main pontoon, he could see someone on the aft deck. He crept out of the side saloon door and came round behind the person, who was now bending down at the corner of the deck. He swept the deck for a second intruder before confronting them.

"What are you doing?" he challenged in an aggressive tone, more out of fear than anything.

The figure turned, saw the knife that Daniel was wielding and let forth a shrill, feminine scream.

Linda, who had been following closely behind Daniel, rushed out on to the deck. At the same time, a man's voice rang out from a boat alongside them.

"What in bloody hell's name do you think you're playing at?"

The man on the next boat jumped over the guard rails and onto the *Lady B*, where he rugby-tackled Daniel to the deck. This caught Daniel completely unaware, and he fell heavily against the fly bridge, the knife flying from his hand as he did so.

Linda, seeing the fight developing, quickly made her way back into the cockpit and locked the door. She went straight to the boat's helm and blew the horn five or six times to try and raise the alarm. Within 30 seconds, people from boats all around were appearing to see what was going on.

Andy, the doctor from the *Southerly*, hopped off of his boat as Linda shouted to him for help. Daniel was finding his strength, and fought back hard against his aggressor while the first intruder continued to scream her head off. Andy came up on deck with the stealth of a cheetah, and soon had Daniel's male attacker in an arm lock.

It was then that Linda saw the two police officers running down the pontoon as fast as their legs would carry them. She released the door and shouted to them that they were being attacked. They leaped straight up onto the boat and went to the aft deck to sort the situation out. One of the police officers restrained Daniel, while the other seized his attacker.

Once he had his breath back, the man shouted, "What the bloody hell is your game? Are you just a fucking idiot, or what?"

"What did you call me?" Daniel yelled, attempting to land another punch.

"All right, watch it, we're police officers. Now how about someone telling me what is going on here?" said the policeman holding Daniel.

Linda was the first to speak. She began to explain what she had awoken to, but the male boarder, who was still being held by the other officer, kept interrupting.

"I've never seen anyone make such a fuss about people tying off before."

The officer, who had introduced himself as PC Thompson earlier, jumped to her defence.

"Well sir, it is the early hours of the morning, which is a hell of a time to be creeping about on someone else's boat. I'm not surprised they were alarmed, I would have been."

"You're obviously not a yachtsman yourself. It happens all the time. We only wanted to tie our boat against theirs!" the man shot back.

PC Thompson sighed. He had been hoping to conclude the incident quickly, and did not want to go into the whys and wherefores of the Cassidy family situation.

"Well, let me put it this way sir. You were on their property when this incident occurred, so I suggest you make your way back to your boat and we forget about it. Before you do, I'd like to see some form of identity from you."

"Are you having a laugh? What sort of police state are we living in now?"

"I'm not going to argue with you, would you please produce some ID?"

With a sigh, the man pulled his wallet out from his inside pocket and produced some credit cards and a membership card with a photo on it. PC Thompson examined them. It appeared that the man was the Labour MP for a London Borough, so he would not be looking for any negative publicity.

"OK. please go back to your boat and forget this ever happened," said PC Thompson.

The man muttered something under his breath, shook himself free from the officer holding him and walked over to where the woman was standing. They made their way back over the guard rails to their own boat.

"I am sorry," Daniel said turning to PC Thompson once they were gone. "I thought—well, I don't know."

"I know what you thought, and I fully understand," said the officer. "What I just can't explain is why they attacked you."

***

That morning, when Linda went to make a drink to take back to bed, she glanced out of the window to see that the boat that had caused the trouble the previous night had already untied and was quietly making her way out of the harbour. This was a relief, as neither she nor Daniel had known how they were going to face them that morning.

"They've gone!" she shouted to Daniel as she picked up her cup of tea.

"Thank God for that!" came his reply from the cabin.

They decided that they would not go on anywhere else. The scare the previous night had dashed any hopes of turning this into a mini holiday; they were simply in hiding. They would head back to Chichester the next day—Daniel wanted to return while the weather was good, as it would have been typical of their recent run of luck if he was unable to make it to the trial because they were stuck in a little harbour.

***

Early on the morning of their departure, Daniel went to visit the duty police officer to tell him they were heading back to Chichester.

The voyage back was uneventful, and before long they were navigating up the Channel to the Chichester marina. Once again, butterflies entered Daniel's stomach at the thought of taking the *Lady B* through the lock, but they locked through without incident and were soon tied up at their berth.

Just as they switched off the engines, Daniel's mobile rang. It was Luke. Daniel sat at the helm seat and brought him up to date, and Luke told him what was happening at work. He and Michelle were apparently due to fly from Singapore that evening. Daniel told him to ring when he got to London and said he would meet him at the office. He was pleased they were both coming over, as they would be able to keep Linda company while Daniel was at the trial.

Daniel and Linda ate dinner on board the boat that evening, having taken Sam for a long walk on the beach in West Wittering. The sea air and the building tension of the lead up to the trial had worn them out, and they were in bed by ten.

***

The alarm went off at 6.30 the following morning, and Daniel was out of bed far quicker than he would normally have been. He had hardly slept, despite his fatigue. Today was the day they would return to their house. They did not mind going back so soon, particularly as Luke and Michelle would be there for moral support and they knew the police would be stationed outside until further notice.

At seven o'clock, the phone rang; Luke was already at the office. Daniel told him they would be there by 11, but it took them twice as long as they had anticipated to pack and unload the boat. On the journey back, Daniel, who had told Luke about the fingerprinting, called Grant. Grant was pleased Luke and Michelle had agreed, and arranged for someone from the local constabulary to go to the office that afternoon and take the prints. He reassured Daniel that once they had them, they could then probably draw some conclusions as to who had broken in to the Cassidy family home

As he hung up, Daniel wondered if that would put their minds to rest or unsettle them further.

CHAPTER 50

When Linda and Daniel finally arrived at the office, the police were on their way out.

"Nice of you to make it!" said Luke with a slightly sarcastic smile. Linda went in first and gave Luke a kiss, followed by Michelle.

"Nice to see you too," remarked Daniel as he followed Linda into the office with Sam in his arms. They shut themselves off in the top office while the General Manager's secretary made them all a coffee. There was much to catch up on. Luke suggested that the girls took one of the rental cars and went down to the house with Sam, but Daniel interjected and said that it wasn't a good idea for them to go on their own. He told Luke and Michelle about the latest situation. Luke agreed that it was probably better for them to all go at once, but Daniel could tell that he thought they were overreacting again.

The girls decided to go off to the pub for lunch with Sam, promising to try to bring back a burger for Daniel and Luke. Once they were gone, the men settled in to talk business, and started by discussing the situation in Singapore. Luke had not worried Daniel with it previously, but business was booming, and it was becoming apparent that things were getting difficult without his presence. Vera was looking after things admirably, but there were many decisions only Luke or Daniel could make, and things were definitely stretching at the seams.

In the UK, it seemed things were all under control, with the management looking after it well. Daniel had been in daily contact to advise on any queries, but his desk was still full of paperwork that needed clearing. He decided he would go through it with Luke that evening, and they would fax Vera to compile replies and quotes for each enquiry that required immediate attention. Daniel was secretly relieved that he had something to take his mind off the following day's events.

By the time the girls arrived back with their burgers, Daniel and Luke had gone through most of the post on their desks, and they all headed back to the house at 4pm that afternoon. Daniel and Linda were apprehensive as they turned into the drive.

"I wonder if it will ever feel the same again. Coming home, I mean," Linda said with a sigh.

"Of course it will, honey, just as soon as this is all behind us."

Parked outside the garage was a blue Ford Focus with two plain-clothed police sat inside. They got out to greet the group.

It was only then that Luke realised the seriousness of the situation confronting his colleague. He had been relatively sheltered from the whole series of events, and at one point had almost scorned Daniel's concerns, but seeing the police sitting outside the house for their protection brought the reality home to him. Daniel noticed a marked change in his attitude towards things that evening. Luke asked about the trial with renewed interest, but Daniel himself tried to guide the conversation away from that, as he was trying to forget it.

They all spent the first couple of hours thoroughly cleaning every inch of the house. It was still covered in fingerprinting dust, and had not been touched since the break in. Once they had finished, they all agreed that it all felt much better, and Linda was relieved that it was home once again.

It was not until about 9pm that Daniel and Luke sat down to go through the paperwork. After a few minutes, Luke announced that he was simply too tired after the flight, so they both agreed to leave it until the following day.

***

The police officers had changed shifts during the night; Daniel had woken to the sound of the second car approaching on the gravel drive, and had heard the muted conversation between the four officers before the original car drove off. He was unable to settle after that, found himself wide-awake by 5am, and was in the kitchen making tea when Luke walked in. He too was wide-awake, but due to jet lag rather than nervous apprehension.

One of the policemen came in to tell Daniel he was going to continue to guard the house while Daniel was in court. While Daniel had said that he would make his own way to the Old Bailey, Grant had insisted that he should be at least accompanied there, if not back. After some discussion, it was agreed that Luke was going to take Daniel and the other officer to the station that morning. Linda had offered to come with them, but Daniel said he would rather go and get it over with on his own.

CHAPTER 51

They left the house at 8am. Daniel's train was leaving at 8.25, and would get into Victoria by 9.30. Daniel said goodbye to Luke as the policeman bought two tickets, and they awaited the arrival of the train. When it arrived, it was already full, and Daniel had to stand for the entire journey.

How do people do this every day? he wondered to himself.

He could see why people suffered the misery of the M25 commuter traffic each day if this was the only other option.

As the train gathered speed pulling out of the station, Daniel looked around to see if there was anyone suspicious nearby. There wasn't, but he felt sure he could have made up a nefarious story for every commuter. Nervously, he held on to the grab rail and pondered what he had in store that day. He wondered if the Old Bailey would be as daunting as it looked on the television, and thought about all the cases he knew of that had been held there, all the notorious criminals that had passed through its doors.

He was torn from his thoughts as the train came to a halt between stations. All the passengers had their noses in books, magazines, or the daily papers, and not a sound could be heard. Daniel looked at his watch. It was already nine o'clock, only 30 minutes to go.

In what seemed like no time at all, they were passing Battersea Power Station. As they rattled over the Thames and on into Victoria, Daniel's nerves were becoming more apparent to him, and his palms were wet.

Once off the train, he made his way down to the tube station, accompanied by the policeman. He already knew he had to take the Circle Line to Liverpool Street, and then change to the Central Line for a couple of stops. The tube was packed, and when the doors opened on the platform, it was all the people on board could do to save themselves from being pushed out. That didn't stop the odd person still trying to board, to the fury of those already on the train.

Shaking his head, Daniel waited patiently. He knew another train would be along shortly.

The journey was quick, and before long he found himself joining the queue at the escalators to take him up to ground level. As he got outside, he looked for a street name so he could get his bearings, and quickly found he was on Newgate Street. After consulting his A-to-Z and conferring with his companion, they set off in the direction of the Old Bailey, arriving at ten to ten exactly. Daniel stopped briefly on the pavement to look up at the imposing building ahead of him.

"I didn't think I'd see the day when I had to enter this place," Daniel commented to the policeman at his side.

"I must admit, you've beaten me to it," he responded with a smile.

They went in through the main entrance and approached the reception counter. He told them of the purpose of his visit, and was told to go to his right, where he was confronted with a glass revolving door. Security ushered him inside. The door closed behind him, leaving him standing enclosed in what looked like an upright torpedo tube. After a few seconds, the door ahead of him opened and he stepped through to the waiting security guards and an area not dissimilar to a Customs hall at an airport. Once through, he was asked which case he was connected with, and shown along a stone-floored corridor with tall ceilings. The corridor was lit by unwelcoming fluorescent tubes, with large wooden doors set at intervals of about 15 feet on the left and small glass-fronted waiting rooms on the right hand side. He was asked if he was for the prosecution or the defence by the young woman accompanying him, and then guided to one of the small waiting rooms, where he took a seat. He was told that counsel would be down to see him shortly.

About half an hour later, just as Daniel was beginning to wonder if he was in the right place, Gill arrived.

"Sorry to have kept you waiting, it's been one of those mornings."

Daniel stood to shake her hand.

"Oh, don't worry!" he said gallantly, trying to hide his apprehension.

"I'm afraid it may be another hour or two until we can bring you in, but I'll pop back shortly to let you know how it's progressing."

"I see. Well I'm not going anywhere," Daniel said meekly, still in awe of his surroundings. As she left, he sat back down on the wooden bench. The following hour seemed like an eternity.

Finally, Grant appeared round the door.

"Hi Daniel. I'm sorry for the delay, we've been having right fun and games upstairs. The jury still hasn't been agreed following some last minute objections from the defence."

Daniel frowned. "Where does that leave us?"

"Well, it's a problem that's unlikely to be resolved today, and even if it is, we've still got to go through the business of swearing them in. All I can suggest is that you return home today, and we'll see you back here at the same time tomorrow. I'm really sorry."

"OK. I'll see you in the morning."

Grant shook hands with Daniel, and then hurriedly disappeared back to the courtroom. Daniel sat back down and took out his train timetable from the pocket of his coat. He decided he would be unable to catch the train that left Victoria in 15 minutes, but would aim to get the one that departed in an hour.

As he walked back through the foyer, he looked for his police escort, who was nowhere to be seen. After checking with the front desk, he discovered the man had been told that Daniel would be in the building for a while, and was off getting a sandwich. He left a message for the policeman to meet him at the train station when he returned. As Daniel turned out of the entrance of the Old Bailey he took his mobile from his pocket and called Linda.

"Hi hon, it's me. Guess what, they've only postponed it until tomorrow!"

"Oh, I am sorry darling, after getting yourself all geared up for it. What a pain!"

"Yeah. I've now got to go through the whole palaver of not knowing what to expect again tomorrow, I suppose. Anyhow, do you think one of you could pick me up at the station an hour and three quarters from now?"

"Of course we can."

"Actually, I can't tell what the delays are going to be like, so I'll give you another call when I'm 15 minutes away. Please make sure someone is in."

"Will do, darling. See you later."

Daniel continued down the street, stopping at a newsagent to pick up a *Daily Telegraph*. Next door was an Italian coffee shop, and as he had half an hour to kill he decided to stop there for a drink before going on to the station.

Inside, there were a few tables down the left hand side opposite the serving counter that opened up to a larger seating area at the back.

Daniel approached the counter and ordered a cappuccino, paid, and carried on to the back of the shop, where there was a lone empty table on the right, just beyond the counter.

He placed his coffee and paper on the table and removed his coat, hanging it over the back of his chair before sitting down and ensuring he had a view of the rest of the café in case he saw the policeman walk past and could stop him.

He tore open the sachet of sugar, emptied the contents into his coffee, and started to stir it. As he did so, the people at the next table left. The movement made Daniel look up, and he froze as something caught his eye.

He blinked, hardly daring to believe what he was seeing. In one fluid motion, he grabbed his *Telegraph* and opened it at eye level, at the same time sinking down in his chair. He allowed himself to glance over the top of the paper as he turned a page, just to ensure he had not been mistaken. He had not. He slowly raised the paper and turned so that he could not be seen from that direction.

Daniel could not believe the predicament in which he now found himself. Opposite him sat Han's mother, the woman he had met in Istanbul, along with two black-haired, moustached, and swarthy-looking characters who Daniel knew he had also seen before, though he couldn't place where. Where was his police escort when he needed him?

Daniel stared at the same spot in his paper, wracking his brains for how he was going to get out of this one. He thought harder about where he had seen the other two before, and at the low rumble of their voices it suddenly came back to him. It was as he had been walking to the toilets, across the foyer of the hotel in Istanbul on the night of Han's mother's birthday.

They could only be there for one reason, and he felt sure it was one of them who had phoned when they had been on the marina at Chichester. It was probably they who had ransacked his home, he realised, and now he had walked straight into them. Daniel looked at his watch; he had about 25 minutes before he needed to leave.

He did not read a word of the paper or even turn a page during the next 25 minutes, but instead began to sweat more and more as the coffee shop emptied, time ticked down, and he realised he was going to have to move.

He had already switched off his mobile so as not to draw attention to himself, fighting the urge to call for help. He knew Han's mother would recognise his voice if she heard it. Although they must have given up on finding him before the trial, he did not want to take the chance of being seen now. He had to move, or not only was he going to miss the train, but it was increasingly likely he would be recognised.

He turned to face the wall as he stood up and placed the paper on the table, not looking in their direction. He spent a while putting his coat on and doing the buttons up, then slid out with his back to them.

"Goodbye sir," the waiter said amicably as Daniel sidled past. Daniel raised his hand and half-smiled in acknowledgement, then slowly turned towards the door. He left the opposite way to which he had come so as not to expose himself to their view, and did not look in, but gazed firmly over the road until he had passed the window. Once he was clear, he looked straight ahead, increased his pace, and headed for the tube station.

He did not look back until he had reached the end of the road, just before he turned the corner on to Ludgate Hill.

His blood ran cold as he saw the three of them had left the café and were heading in his direction.

He adopted a half-jog until he reached the next turning into St. Paul's Churchyard. When he glanced back, there was no sign of the trio.

Daniel found himself glancing back every few hundred yards as he walked to the tube station. He walked towards one end of the platform, where he stood and waited anxiously for the tube that would take him towards Victoria. The tube arrived, and as he was boarding he glanced toward the platform entrance and saw a man heading rapidly in his direction. Thankfully, the doors closed before his pursuer had time to board.

Daniel was pleased to see that the carriage was fairly empty. He jumped on, walked to a series of empty seats, and sat down.

As he arrived at Victoria, he realised he had only four minutes to catch his train. He bolted up the escalators, then up the stairs into the main station, scanning for his platform number. It was down the far end to the right. He jogged across the station, glancing at his watch every few seconds until he reached the platform, where the guard had just reached the end of the train and had been about to blow the whistle.

"Wait!" shouted Daniel as he ran up to the end carriage.

"You'll have to wait for the next one, son!" the guard shouted, before he blew his whistle.

"Like hell I will!" said Daniel, fighting annoyance. The train was not yet moving, Daniel was the only one on the platform, and the guard could have waited three more seconds. He yanked open the door closest to him and jumped on, slamming it behind him as the train started to shunt forwards. He heard the shouts of annoyance from the guard outside, but he did not care. The train was safely on the move, and he was on his way.

***

Han had gradually resigned himself to the fact that whatever was said in court would have to be. His barrister had reiterated on each visit how necessary it was to let the process run its course, and Maya had gone back to Istanbul, saying she would return for the trial, but not before. She had had enough of him.

In light of the fact that his friends had given up looking for Daniel, Han had asked them to make sure his mother was all right. She had already visited him soon after his arrest, and had given him a real dressing down when she heard about his treatment of his wife. He had felt thoroughly ashamed. She and Maya were close to each other, and when it came to the crunch Han's mother was firmly on Maya's side, and deplored the way Han behaved toward her.

***

Fifteen minutes from home, Daniel phoned to let them know where he was. Luke had offered to come and pick him up, and Linda said she would make sure he left immediately.

Daniel spent that afternoon with going through various items of business that needed sorting out, sending at least 22 emails and 15 faxes that were long overdue. Without Daniel's undivided attention, things had definitely been beginning to slip, and as he had warned, the growth of the company was more than Luke could cope with alone.

Daniel slept fitfully that night, his mind filled with visions of the Old Bailey and images of what the main courtroom must look like. He was dreading facing Han in court.

CHAPTER 52

The next morning, they followed the same pattern and duly arrived at the Old Bailey at ten to ten. Daniel once again thanked the policeman who had accompanied him on the journey—having apologised profusely for the confusion when they had been reunited back at the house the day before—and was duly shown into the same waiting room.

Within three minutes, Gill appeared, bid him good morning, and asked him to follow her upstairs to the courts.

They ascended the stairs to an enormous hall with a high ceiling and entrances to the main courtrooms down one side. There was a series of rigid plastic chairs arranged about twenty feet away from each door, all empty except for a couple outside Court 2 they stopped in front of.

"You're the first witness for the prosecution, so you should be called in about fifteen minutes or so," Gill advised Daniel, waiting for him to nod his acceptance before disappearing through the door.

Daniel sat down and retrieved his book. He started to read, although he found concentrating difficult through the questions swirling his mind.

Is there a small briefing room before you get to the main court, I wonder?

Yes, surely there must be. I hope they brief me on the form; who is who and how to address everyone. Surely they must. Oh well, I'll soon find out.

He was pulled from his thoughts as Gill stuck her head out into the hall. "Daniel?" she called, "I'm afraid you're on."

"Oh well, let's get it over with," he muttered, though his legs were turning to jelly and there was a churning sensation in his stomach. He followed Gill through the doors. As he walked in, he was startled to find all eyes were upon him.

"Would you step into the witness box?" said a clerk.

As he made his way over, Daniel started to look around him, working out who was sitting where. It was a daunting place. His gaze eventually landed on the back row to his left, opposite the judge. Han sat with his head bowed and eyes closed. Daniel quickly averted his gaze and looked up at the judge to his right, the jury directly opposite him, and then at the barristers. He could not yet work out who was working for who, but was sure it would all soon be made clear.

He spotted Grant and Gill sitting at one of the tables towards the front of the court, so assumed that the prosecution barrister was the one in front of them. The clerk walked into the box behind Daniel, and having confirmed which religion he followed, handed him a Bible. He told Daniel to hold it in his right hand and repeat the words printed on a card he held up.

"Please speak clearly into the microphone, Mr Cassidy."

"I hereby promise to tell the truth, the whole truth..." Daniel spoke clearly and concisely into the microphone, reciting the lines as if on autopilot. As he finished, he heard the sound of a woman crying from above him. He looked up, but could not see anything. He realised it could have been Maya, and suddenly felt awful for being there.

He was asked to confirm his name and address for the record, and did so. After that, three of the barristers in the row closest to him promptly introduced themselves.

Daniel had got the prosecution barrister right, but was thrown by the fact that two people were actually on trial, Han and someone called Eugene, represented by the centre barrister.

The prosecution barrister started by asking general questions.

"How did Mr Atima initially make contact with you, Mr Cassidy?"

"At the boat show in Earls Court, London, via information from a colleague of his in Singapore."

"What was the nature of his enquiry?"

"Well, he initially wanted to see if he could build boats for us in Turkey, but the nature of the inquiry changed. He wanted to know if we wished to purchase sports boats from him."

"How did he propose that business be conducted if you were interested?"

"He wanted to supply the boats free of charge, and for the profit to be split when they were sold on."

"Was this unusual, in your opinion?"

"Yes, it is certainly a way of business that is new to me. If anything, most suppliers normally insist on full payment up front, before the goods are shipped."

"Can you tell us about your trip to Istanbul?"

Daniel went on to tell the story of his visit. He kept to facts, omitting the detail of his inner feelings and suspicions. When he glanced up, he locked eyes with Han who was in view just above the barrister's head. He was staring at Daniel with a cold, unmoved expression. It sent a shiver down Daniel's spine, and from that moment on he made sure he did not regain eye contact.

"Why did you insist on going to Istanbul?" the prosecution continued.

"We had to know what the quality of the boats was like. We couldn't just trade blind, even if they were being supplied free of charge."

"What were your findings when you got there?"

"Well, quite frankly, the quality of the boats was nowhere near good enough."

The questions from the prosecution kept coming from for a further two and a half hours, and only ceased when the judge intervened to suggest that they broke for lunch. A clerk confirmed Daniel's suspicions that he would have to be in the witness box for the afternoon as well.

As they left, Gill told Daniel that he could go to the restaurant on the top floor for some lunch, but that he should be back ready for court at 2pm sharp.

Daniel wandered up to the top floor and found the restaurant. He looked around him warily the whole time, hyper-aware that some of Han's relations could be in the vicinity and knowing he would have to avoid them at all costs. He wasn't sure whether they would have access to this part of the building or not, but he would keep an eye open anyway.

He sat alone eating a lunch of Irish stew and pondered the morning's events. He felt the afternoon would be easier now he knew the ropes, but the vision of Han staring coldly and deliberately in the dock kept coming back to him.

He finished his stew, went to collect a coffee, and then sat back at his table to call Linda, who picked up the phone almost before it had rung.

"How's it going sweetheart? Have you finished?"

"No, unfortunately it looks like I'm in for the afternoon as well."

"I've been thinking about you all morning, are you OK?"

"Yes honey, I'm fine. There's not much to it really, just standing there answering questions."

"Can you see him from where you are giving evidence?"

"Yes, I'm afraid I can. Anyhow, I'll bring you fully up to date this evening. I'd better get back down there for the next session."

He hung up and made his way back down to the court, where he once again settled outside. At ten past two, he was asked to re-enter the witness box.

The prosecution continued their questioning for a further half an hour, and it was then the turn of the defence. The first questions were essentially a re-run of the questions that had been asked by the prosecution, but phrased slightly differently. After a few minutes, the tack changed.

"I put it to you, Mr Cassidy, that your dealings were predominantly not with my client, but with a gentleman in Singapore who was really behind all this."

From across the courtroom, Grant looked at Gill. "Here we go," he murmured.

"No," said Daniel, without hesitation. "In fact, nearly all my dealings with reference to the boats were with Han. The other guy knew nothing about them whatsoever."

"Well, I would suggest that the fact he knew nothing about boats at all is highly irrelevant, considering it was his intention to smuggle drugs, not boats. Could you confirm that you did in fact deal with someone else regarding the boats?"

"Yes, we dealt with both of them."

"Thank you, Mr Cassidy. I would now like to move on to the way in which you do business normally, and to establish why this offer of business from my client was so different, in your opinion. How do you normally conduct your business?"

Daniel spent the next half-hour explaining the different types of shipping and methods of payment they used for different products from different places. By the end of it, Daniel had irrefutably shown how odd the offer of business the Turk had made was.

David spent the next hour trying to persuade Daniel that his trip to Turkey had been entirely normal, but Daniel stuck to his guns, determined to demonstrate otherwise.

By 4.30pm, the defence had finished with Daniel and the judge announced that the trial would adjourn until tomorrow. Grant and Gill caught up with him in the large foyer afterwards.

"Thank you so much, Daniel," Grant said as he shook his hand. "I don't think they will call you again, but you're staying in the UK for a while anyway, I understand?"

"Yes, that's right. Unfortunately an aunt of Linda's is not too well, so we'll be staying for a bit to support her mother. We'll be here for a couple of weeks at least."

"OK. Well, we'll be in touch if there's any news, but as far as you're concerned I think the answer is to try and forget the whole ordeal."

"Thank you, but I really would appreciate knowing what happens."

"Don't worry, you'll be one of the first to know, but this could go on for a month or two."

"I'm sure you won't have any trouble finding me to let me know," Daniel said with a grin.

As Daniel turned and walked from the Old Bailey, it was as if an enormous weight had been lifted from his shoulders. He felt like a new man. As he sat on the train at Victoria, he was suddenly overcome with tiredness. Now the stress had lifted, it was a real struggle to stay awake, but he managed. He once again phoned home as the train was approaching, and Luke came to collect him from the station.

CHAPTER 53

When Daniel walked through the front door, he was pleased to find that Linda and Michelle had put a couple of bottles of Moet on ice. Over the course of the evening, the four of them drank a great deal too much of it. They were delighted that the trial was over for them, and they could regain their normal lives once again.

The following morning, they phoned Hong Kong with an update. Keanu answered, and was delighted to hear it was all over. He said he and Kate would arrange to visit Daniel and Linda in Singapore as soon as they were home.

**

Turning their attention to family matters, Daniel and Linda spent the next few days with Daniel's parents, and were there when Linda's aunt died peacefully a week later. They stayed for the funeral, heading back to Singapore a couple of days after that. On the plane, they talked at length about the fact that Edward Lim was probably still at large, but they felt sure that they could resume normal life nonetheless. Linda rested her head on Daniel's shoulder, and joked that life was probably going to be a little dull after all the recent excitement

"Yes, and I'm looking forward to every moment of it," Daniel responded warmly.

"So am I."

***

True to his word, Daniel threw himself into catching up with office work over the next week, although he left at four each afternoon to ensure he could spend some time with Sam before he went to bed. Linda was pleased to be able to resume her normal social activities and their couples dinners; suddenly, both she and Daniel were in great demand because of what they had been through.

Two weeks later, Keanu and Kate came to stay. It was a week of total relaxation and leisure, with water skiing, tennis, and dining top of the agenda, mixed in with shopping for the girls, who must have known every paving slab in Orchard Road by the time they had finished.

It was during that week, after discussions with Keanu, that Daniel phoned the officer who had been in charge of the operation in Singapore out of sheer curiosity. He asked if they had found anyone in connection with the drugs running.

"No, not directly," the man replied. "However a character we picked up in Malaysia who was at the identity parade in Kuala Lumpur proved to be quite interesting, and has been put away by the Malaysian police for a long time. I have to say, I wouldn't be surprised if any drugs connections with Mr Lim stopped when he went away, but that is purely, as you say in England, a hunch. I'm pleased it is over for you, Mr Cassidy, it was not a pleasant thing to have been involved with, I expect."

"No, you could put it that way. Thanks for your support."

***

A month after returning, Daniel rang Grant to see if there had been any news on the trial. He was surprised to hear that it was still ongoing.

"What on earth is that costing the taxpayer?" he asked incredulously.

"You don't want to know," came Grant's response, "but it will be worth it when he's put away."

"I will be back in London in a couple of weeks' time, so maybe I'll give you a ring then?"

"Yes, do. I should be in a better position to estimate the end of it by then."

"OK Grant, speak to you then."

***

After a couple of uneventful weeks, Daniel and Luke set off for a week-long visit to London, most of which was set to be taken up with meetings at the UK office. They were due to talk to a number of importers in various European countries who were keen to become sole agents for their products.

On the Tuesday morning after his arrival, Daniel's mobile rang. It was Grant.

"Daniel, hi. How are you doing?"

"I'm fine thank you, Grant. You've obviously got some news."

"Yes. I wondered if Gill and I could buy you a drink this evening and let you know how it all worked out?"

"Sure, where do you suggest?"

"How about the little pub close to your office?"

"The Hatch? OK that's fine. I'll be finished here at about six, so shall we say 6.15?"

"See you then Daniel."

"OK, but—?"

Before he could ask for details, Grant had already hung up. Daniel toyed with the idea of ringing him back, but decided it was only a few hours until he found out anyway, so he'd wait until the evening.

He left the office with Luke at exactly 6pm, and they duly arrived at the Hatch at ten past. Grant and Gill were already there, ordering their drinks.

"Ah, Daniel!" Grant said, offering a hand as they approached. "Hi, Luke. How are you?"

Daniel thought he detected a false happiness in his voice, but let the thought go until he knew better.

"What can I get you both?" Grant offered.

"Half a Strongbow for me, please," Daniel replied.

"And a pint of orange juice for me," Luke added.

The barman poured the drinks and they wandered over to the nearest table. Once they were all seated, Grant initiated the conversation, "Right, where shall I start?"

"All I really need to know is how long he's gone down for," Daniel suggested helpfully.

"We'll get to that," said Gill. "You need to know what happened after you left the courtroom first."

"Well, he put in a plea for duress," Grant started.

"That doesn't mean a thing to me."

"Basically, he knew he had been caught red-handed, so he did the only thing he could and claimed that he did the drug smuggling because the lives of his family were under threat, as well as his own."

"Under threat from whom?" Daniel quizzed Grant.

"Well, this is where it gets interesting. He denied he had a partner in the operation, but said he had no option but to do it because the supplier was forcing him to."

"Surely if that was the case he would have to prove it?"

"Logically, yes, but he wasn't asked to and we couldn't disprove it. The jury believed him, and it was an easy out."

"Wait a minute, are you telling me what I think you're telling me? Someone who was caught with thirty million pounds' worth of heroin in his hands has just *walked free*?"

Gill nodded. "I can assure you that we're as upset about it as anyone. You can imagine the months of work that it has taken to put this whole case together."

"I certainly can."

"Unbelievable!" Luke said, shaking his head.

"Yes, Luke, it is." Grant replied. "We're completely gutted by it, but at the end of the day we did stop a large consignment of drugs from hitting the streets. Regardless, it's not the result we would like to have seen, or indeed the one we expected. He really got off on a technicality; if he had had to prove it, he wouldn't be free now."

Daniel was dumbstruck. Even when he found his voice, all he could say was, "Well, if it's that easy to get away with a stunt like that, he's probably engineering the second attempt right now."

"I don't think we'll be seeing any more of our friend, thanks to the shock of it all. In any case, there will be people in Turkey who will be out for his blood," Grant remarked.

Daniel nodded in half-hearted agreement, and the four of them sat in silence for a few seconds as Daniel and Luke let the latest information sink in. They were genuinely confused.

As they parted ways shortly afterwards, Daniel quietly wondered to himself whether Han's friends had achieved more than they were all aware of. Had they managed to intimidate the jury? When he mentioned it to Luke, he said he wondered exactly the same thing.

Han walked out into the grey, dreary light, tears of relief in his eyes. *Thank goodness for the British justice system.*

Han, Maya, his mother and his two colleagues all shared a celebratory meal at their hotel that evening. His room was a far cry from the prison cell of the previous night, and he had never appreciated a bed so much in his life.

The following day, having flown back to Istanbul, Han and Maya drove out to their home on the outskirts of the city. It felt good to be back; there had been a time when he had thought he might never see it again.

He walked out on to the patio and drew deeply on his cigarette, looking out over the garden in the fading evening light. He noticed the lawn needed cutting. That was a job he would be more than happy to do tomorrow. He had learned his lesson; had it not been for the lawyers his mother had engaged, he might never have had the chance to cut that grass again. He vowed to lead a quieter life, and only wondered where Xu had vanished.

Just then, something glinted briefly in the shrubbery at the foot of the garden.

A piece of glass, perhaps? He stared at the spot for a second. Something was moving...

Horrified, he turned to throw himself sideways, but he was a fraction of a second too late. A sharp crack echoed across the garden, and the high-velocity bullet caught him in the middle of the chest. He collapsed across the edge of the patio, his mouth agape, and his eyes caught in a frozen stare of shock. His cigarette fell from his fingers, rolled off the edge of the patio, and dropped, still glowing, into the rich green grass.

Printed in Poland
by Amazon Fulfillment
Poland Sp. z o.o., Wrocław

53830121R00216